Designing and Printing Textiles

June Fish

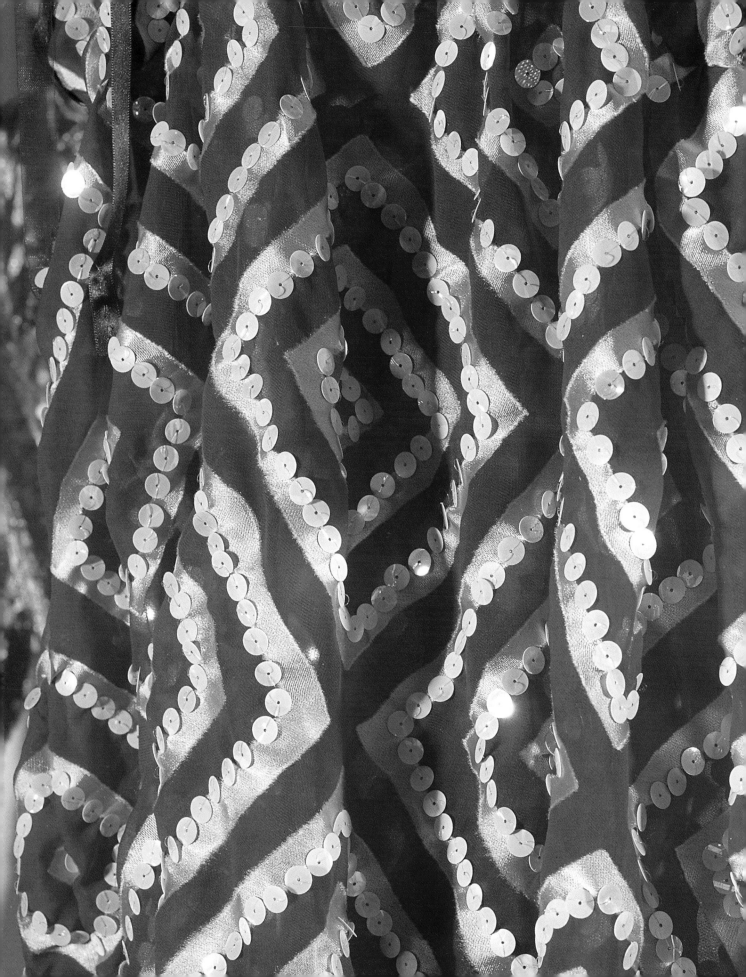

Designing and Printing Textiles

June Fish

The Crowood Press

First published in 2005 by
The Crowood Press Ltd
Ramsbury, Marlborough
Wiltshire SN8 2HR

www.crowood.com

British Library Cataloguing-in-Publication Data
A catalogue record for this book is available from the British Library.

ISBN 1 86126 776 2

Illustration previous page: Detail of sequinned lingerie collection, by Tamara Boyle.

Cover illustration: 'Ilas Cositas', a silk screen printed soda ash devoré on silk/metallic mix.
Artist: Amanda French (frenchamanda@hotmail.com)

Acknowledgements
The Author would like to thank Central St Martins Art College and the Dean Jane Rapley, for allowing me the time to research the book. Thank you to the staff on the Textile's course for offering advice, information and proof reading, particularly Sarah Wilson, Garth Lewis, Bec Chivers, Anne Smith, Deborah Peasgood, Linsay Robinson, Rodney Wilson and Kevin Bolger. A big thank you to the students for allowing me to photograph their work, and the staff at the College Archive for their assistance.

Also thanks to Helen Sykes for her editing skills, Brewster for allowing use of their project brief, George Zacal at CWV Wallpapers, Elaine English at Middlesex University, and Beatrice Mayfield for an insight into the Crafts Council.

Thanks to Tim Marshall for the photography work.

Disclaimer
All efforts have been made to contact and trace companies and designers for images of historical works donated to the Central St Martins College Archive that appear in the book. In some cases this has not been possible, so only work produced over a certain time limit has been used visually.

Typefaces used: text, Stone Sans; headings, Frutiger; chapter headings, Rotis Sans.

Typeset and designed by
D & N Publishing
Lowesden Business Park, Hungerford, Berkshire.

Printed and bound in Singapore by Craft Print International Ltd.

CONTENTS

INTRODUCTION

Digitally printed textile design, based on a landscape garden theme, by Aya Tsukai.

The aim of this book is to offer direction and advice across the whole process of designing for surface pattern and textiles. This includes identifying the design components necessary to create innovative designs, and how then to produce them practically on fabric. The book is written at a level to appeal to students, designers and enthusiasts, who may want to follow the process from start to finish, or simply dip into different sections when needed.

To make a sustainable career in this field requires all-round ability. This includes researching skills, designing to a high standard, and having an established market you can provide goods or designs for. The Crafts Council in their leaflet, *Supporting Makers*, states some key points they look for when offering grants to new designers including:

- Quality of ideas/concepts
- Originality of design
- Consistency and integrity of voice
- Quality of making and technical skill
- Commitment to the development of your practice
- Understanding of the context and sector in which the work will be placed
- Understanding and exploration of materials used
- Extent to which the applicant has researched their equipment needs
- Consideration of the market for their work and the running of the business.

This is aimed at designers setting up their own practice, but many of the criteria listed apply to all levels of work whether you are a student starting out, a hobbyist, or already working within a design company.

Wallpaper design from the 1950s by Line.

The textile industry is very competitive, so keep a broad view of areas in which to sell your work, and develop your possible career options. It is not uncommon for designers who prefer making one-off commissions to also produce collections of commercial design work, or go into teaching, to aid with financing their career, or providing another outlet for exchanging ideas. Surface pattern also crosses over into illustration, ceramics and architecture, as well as fashion and interior textiles, and there may be opportunities for exciting collaborations.

Essentially your work is there to be seen by others, so always find an outlet for showing your work and obtaining feedback, otherwise you are unlikely to move on and develop creatively. Always keep generating new design ideas as potential buyers will want to see new ranges of work, and present yourself in the most professional way possible. The back of the book lists organizations and magazines that can help advise you on improving your professionalism, and keep you in touch with job and exhibition opportunities, and possible grants and schemes. *Designing and Printing Textiles* also aims to give strong practical direction for those wishing to replicate their paper design work onto fabric. Many students and designers often find this a stumbling block, as they have less experience and control when working onto fabric, and can lose the creative spark found in their paper work. Chapter 3 links and overlaps these two areas introducing interchangeable methods, and breaks down those barriers. This also includes broadening your use of materials and tools to create more innovative and experimental designs.

To sell textile goods or samples, care needs to be taken over the quality of the finished pieces, particularly if they are for a functional use. Fabric types, dyes and printing and painting methods all need due consideration, to prevent mistakes and less than permanent results that can be costly. The recipes for dyeing and printing are intended to be as straightforward as possible, for those who are inexperienced. The materials are easily accessible and take into account consideration of health and safety issues.

Finally, all textile designers should be aware of issues currently topical in the textile industry, as they will eventually affect your future. Environmental and sustainable textiles, new ways of applying pattern using developing technology and fabrics, and the future use of traditional methods are all touched on, and may become an area of interest.

CHAPTER 1

SOURCING IDEAS AND RESEARCHING SURFACE PATTERN

How to Start

As a designer, creating original ideas and sourcing imagery is often the most exciting and stimulating part of a project. Researching in depth will really pay off at the design and making stage, as you will have a huge pool of information to draw on. This chapter will give you some practical starting points on researching imagery and exploring ways of interpreting your ideas on paper. A sound background knowledge of surface pattern design history is also important to add depth to your research, and some key design periods are listed in this section. Finding a niche in which to exhibit or sell your work is also part of the researching process, and this chapter will look at potential ways of exhibiting and selling your work in a relevant market.

Sourcing Imagery

The imagery, colour and materials that combine to make innovative and original patterns and prints can come from virtually any source, and will often be completely unrelated to conventional ideas for surface pattern and textiles. Whether it is a look at alternative crafts and cultures from around the world, a delve into history, or a reflection of contemporary trends, a natural

**Traditional floral wallpaper design by Edward Pond.
(Central St Martins Museum and Study Collection)**

or organic theme, or the man-made and artificial, all these and more can provide the beginning to create exciting designs.

Your starting point may be a representation of your own personal unique experiences and thoughts. Even commercial briefs may forecast, for example, a trend based on childhood experiences for inspiration. The fine arts can also set trends for design disciplines, and in textiles, particularly, the work of painters is influential because of their use of form and colour. Fine artists have often produced collections of work for the textile market, based on their painting or drawing style. Also remember to look beyond art and design, as inspiration can be found from other creative disciplines such as literature, philosophy and science.

Some designers and makers find the actual materials and processes involved in making textiles and other craft disciplines is the starting point from which their ideas and themes develop, and they let the materials and processes dictate the finished pattern. A textile dyer, for example, may create random patterns from experimental methods of resist dyeing, and the overlaying of colours to come to an end patterned result.

As well as developing your creative ideas, you should also begin thinking about how your designs will be viewed practically; one of the main reasons for designing is for others to see and experience your work.

The best way of researching this area is to go out and look at what other printed textile and surface pattern designers are doing. Even if you are compromising your design work for the more commercial market, it is still a useful guide. It is important not to become isolated particularly if you no longer have a student support network, or are not working in a shared design studio. Visiting design exhibitions and end-of-year shows at colleges, and looking at design books and magazines will

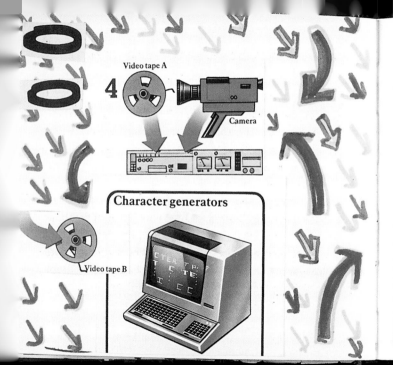

4 Video tape A

Camera

Character generators

Video tape B

RADIO ASTRONOMY

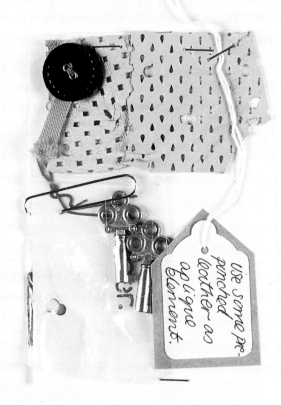

Use some pre-punched leather as appliqué elements.

Leather

Bronze leather. Cuts easily, contrasting weight to paper.

OPPOSITE PAGE
TOP: **Sketchbook research by June Fish.**

BOTTOM: **Sketchbook research by Nadia Parsons.**

BELOW:
Sketchbook designs by Natalie Hand.

keep you inspired and aware of what is currently going on around you.

If you are working towards an end-product for either the fashion or furnishing industry, visits to the shops, trade fairs, and a look at fashion and furnishing books and magazines such as *International Textiles* and *Textile View*, will provide you with inspiration on current trends. An organization such as the

Crafts Council has a resource centre, website and bookshop, where designers and designer makers can see current exhibitions, new books and magazines, and seek advice on design and business issues. This provides a valuable source of networking as well as practical and financial support, and possible avenues for exhibiting work.

Many of the boundaries between disciplines such as fine art and textiles have now blurred, so keep your horizons broad, as the need to find new ways of interpreting pattern means that methods, materials and disciplines are continually crossed over to evolve new design ideas. Later on in this chapter, we will look more at defining the market you wish to work in.

Collating Material

SKETCHBOOK

The first step is to buy a sketchbook or at the least an exercise book where you can collate the beginnings of your source material. Make notes of any ideas that pop into your head, (even if only a word) or they will easily be forgotten. If you enjoy sketching or painting, it is worth investing in a good quality cartridge paper sketchbook (140 to 150g/sm acid free) to make a record of any inspiring images along the way. Try to remember to take it wherever you go; holidays often produce the most inspiring source material.

Sketchbooks range in size, so a smallish A5-size book may be worth carrying around with you, and a larger A4 or A3 book is worth having at home to expand your ideas further. Even established designers working to tight commercial briefs keep collecting and cataloguing new material, as it may be relevant in future projects.

DRAWING AND PAINTING MATERIALS

It is worth sourcing out a good art shop, or mail order through the Internet (addresses can be found at the back), as art materials can be expensive. If you are a student, many art shops provide a student discount. Listed below are some basic materials that may be useful to start with. Keep an open mind and try things out, don't get stuck in a certain way of working with the same materials even if it is a successful formula. Versatility is a good asset for a commercial designer, and different materials and ways of applying them will suit particular themes for a commercial brief. If you are experimental at the start, you won't get stuck in a rut later on, where you find it hard to break out of your regular formula.

Hand-printed and digitally printed functional shapes for a contemporary interior space,
based on the previous sketchbook designs (*see* p.11), by Natalie Hand.

BEGINNERS' MATERIALS

- Sketching pencils, ranging from hard to soft – HB, B, 2B, 3B, 4B, 5B, 6B

- Putty rubber

- Sharpener and scalpel

- Ruler

- Felt tips

- Fountain ink pen, or dip pen

- Colour pencils (Caran Dache are useful as they can be used with water to create a water-colour effect)

- Gouache paints (a versatile range of paints, 8–10 colours)

- Paintbrushes (sable brushes are superior in quality, but nylon would be sufficient to begin with. Try a variety of sizes, shapes and widths)

- Pastels (chalk and oil will both need a fixative spray. Oil pastels can be used with turpentine to create a more painterly effect)

- Indian, watercolour inks (a vibrant colour range that can be bleached back into)

- Paper glue (for collage)

- Scissors

- Sponges (for paint washes)

CAMERA

A good camera is also incredibly useful particularly if you find drawing difficult or you do not have enough time to sketch, especially at places you are unlikely to visit again. A digital camera also means that you can manipulate the images on computer as part of the designing process.

Going one step further, if you are lucky enough to have access to a photographic dark room, then it is also possible to use photographic or light sensitive paper and expose and develop the images of solid objects directly onto the paper. This method only works with black and white photographic paper. You will need to lay the objects on the paper and expose them to light, creating a photogram.

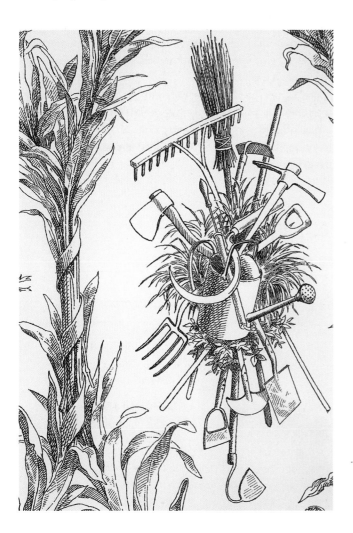

Wallpaper design using a cross-hatched drawing technique, by Belinda Gordon Davis, for Shand Kydd Focus. (By kind permission of CWV Group Ltd)

How to Interpret your Research

Your sketchbook is there to quickly note down your ideas, collate visual images, produce drawn roughs and to try out different forms of mark making. It doesn't matter if the results are left unclear or unfinished; the more variety and spontaneity in your sketchbook the more exciting and stimulating it will become, and you will begin to draw out potential design ideas. It is worth collaging and pasting in photographs, magazine pictures, postcards and photocopies from books, by cutting purposefully and also tearing randomly, interspersing the images together. You can then sketch and paint from sections of the collages or work right over the top of them in drawing or painting media.

Sketching and painting from life is also invaluable, as you are immediately interpreting the image in your own personal way of seeing things in your own drawing style. If you have not been formally trained at college, it may be worth while enrolling on a short course in drawing and painting from life to strengthen and broaden your abilities, so that you can visualize your ideas much easier.

If you have not used many art materials before or done much drawing, below is a selection of mark-making and drawing techniques you can try out.

Try drawing with pencils of different levels of hardness and softness, using a variety of lines and marks, including:

- Dots – build up concentrated areas of dots to represent depth and shade.
- Hatching – where lines are used to create a shading effect, and are all drawn in one direction, becoming more frequent to represent heavy shade.
- Cross-hatching – the same as above, but the lines are criss-crossed.
- Shading – use a softer pencil in heavier areas to add shade and depth, this could even be purposeful scribble.
- Erasing – on already heavily shaded areas use your eraser to draw back in, creating a negative mark.
- Linear drawing – practise drawing outlines, and minimizing the marks needed to create a recognizable image.
- Blending – once you have drawn shaded areas, use a cloth to blur the pencil marks to create all-over gentle shading.

Charcoal, pastels, ink pen and fibre-tip pens can also create these effects in a looser fashion. You may find it hard to work on a smaller scale with bolder materials, but you can work on larger pieces and scale the images down on a photocopier or by scanning them onto a computer to fit the size required.

If you have a good selection of paints and inks, then experiment with different marks and textures using a range of brushes and painting implements. Gouache paints are the best investment, as they can paint flat opaque colour, and can also be watered down to create a more translucent effect (*see* Chapter 3 for information on suitable paper).

Experiment with the transparency and solidity of your colours. Use watercolour, gouache or watered down inks to create washes. Wetting the paper first adds to the effect, or use a pipette to drop splashes of ink onto wet areas. A spray diffuser, or even flicking ink off a toothbrush, will create a speckled effect.

Textures can be created by applying thicker paint either with bold brush strokes, sponges or by stippling or dragging the paint across the paper. If you wish to use a thicker paint other than gouache, then try acrylic or oil paint. Alternatively, rather than using conventional methods of applying paint, interesting textures can be made using crumpled paper or foil, serrated cardboard, and bubble wrap to transfer the paint medium onto your paper.

For more 3D effects, PVA glue can be applied to thicken the paint surface, and used to trap layers of tissue papers, string or easily glueable objects, that can then be painted over.

A negative of a drawn image can be achieved by applying a reasonably thick layer of paint onto paper, and then drawing back into it with a scalpel, pencil, brush handle or another reasonably sharp edge, quickly, before the paint dries.

Wax and masking fluid can be drawn onto paper to act as a resist and to protect the surface when painted over with ink and paint. Wax crayons can be used to make rubbings of a textured object underneath such as tree bark (this is called frottage), and when a wash is applied over the top, the texture will show through.

Masking fluid can be painted directly onto your paper with a ruling pen, and left to dry. Once dry, paint or draw over the fluid, and when the paint is dry, gently rub off the masking fluid revealing the clean protected surface underneath. Masking fluid can also act as a barrier to keep colours separate while they dry, before the fluid is removed. (*See* Chapter 3 for further techniques.)

Remember to integrate different media and techniques together. A fine linear drawing technique can be applied over a background wash, or a paper collage and so on. Experimenting leads to unexpected results that you can go onto and develop and personalize.

Abstract painted and textured design, by Sharifa Syed-Hahar.

Sources on Inspiration and Background Research in Surface Pattern

Two of the common themes in commercial trends and forecasts for textiles are reinterpreting historical design styles, and using influences from ethnic cultures. Both are often combined. The deadline for a commercial brief will often be short, and you will need to find and access material quickly. As a designer, it is important to develop a strong background knowledge of the history and development of design, and gain easy familiarity with a variety of cultural and ethnic styles. The broader and more sophisticated your knowledge becomes, the more evolved and fresh your pattern ideas will be.

It is worth beginning by studying and redrawing historically established surface pattern designs, from books, museums or galleries. By doing this, you will develop a greater understanding of how different pattern formations are structured and what materials were used, and begin to identify motifs and regular pattern systems that are related to particular cultures and eras. Try collaging and mixing different patterns together in your drawings, to see if you can develop the pattern structures.

Surface pattern can be traced back to ancient civilizations, and if you live near a museum of ancient history or have visited ancient archaeological sites, a wealth of inspiring patterned designs can be found. These include Roman mosaics, Grecian friezes and ceramics, Islamic tiles, Byzantine manuscripts and mosaics, Egyptian hieroglyphics, Chinese calligraphy, African jewellery and costumes, and Celtic art to name but a few. Many of these pattern traditions still carry on today. Reinterpretations of ancient designs can be seen throughout history, and when combined with contemporary ideas of the day create something entirely different. Art and design movements from the twentieth century such as Art Deco can trace their influences back to Ancient South American and Egyptian influences, the latter becoming popular after the opening of Tutankamen's tomb in 1922. This, combined with the design and industrial advances of the 1920s and 1930s, created a unique design movement.

Art galleries, national museums, furniture and craft museums, and specific touring exhibitions, help provide a historical link in surface pattern, through depictions of fashion, interiors and architecture, evoking the colour themes and styles of those periods in question. Specialist books and catalogues will delve much deeper into particular historical visual images you may be interested in, and it is worth gradually building up a personal collection of books to refer back to in the future, or at least photocopied images from library books that are a basis for inspiration. This is very important for a textile designer, as historical motifs and styles are cyclical, and are continually reused and updated in contemporary design.

Fabric swatch from a pattern book of 1867. (Central St Martins Museum and Study Collection)

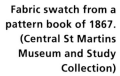

A History of Patterning

Some of the earliest traders in textiles were the Chinese who exported silks overland, before silk was cultivated in other areas, such as the Byzantine Empire, which became an important textile producer with its position bridging the East and West. As soon as trade routes opened from Europe to Asia and the Middle East, influences from national cultures around the world began to be seen and then incorporated into European-style design. Key periods were the late Middle Ages when the maritime cities of Italy traded with the East; and the beginnings of trading followed by the colonialization of Asia and Africa, by several European nations.

Most mass-produced printed textiles come from the nineteenth century onwards with the start of industrialization, and reflect the beginning of the textile industry as it is today. At this time, France, England and the USA produced the most cloth, French design was the most influential and England took many ideas from France, the best known French producer of textiles being from Joy. The resultant materials, called '*Toile de Joy*', produced conversational images of historic and pastoral scenes that are still reproduced today.

The opening of trade routes led to a hybrid of design styles, and many important ethnic designs were reinterpreted for Western use, often losing their initial cultural value along the way.

In Great Britain, the Victoria and Albert Museum was opened in 1857, which collated many examples of design from around the globe, providing visual inspiration for designers. The archive is still available to look at today.

Wallpaper design in a Chinese style by Korin Peter Sumner, for Shand Kydd Focus. (By kind permission of CWV Group Ltd)

Ethnic Design Influences

Traditional ethnic art and design is still widely used in commercial surface pattern today; and traditional print and dye processes from other cultures have been widely adopted for craft-making purposes. Below is a generic selection of sources for historical ethnic patterning that you may find useful:

India and Pakistan. India was also one of the earliest traders in textiles, as evidence of trade with Ancient Egypt has been found. India and Pakistan are both influential for their range of embroidered and appliquéd patterns. Block printing was also prevalent, but eventually could not compete with modern European methods. The paisley image that is Indian in origin is a classic motif, used in Western design. Indian chintzes have also been influential and redesigned for Western use.

China and Japan. Chinoiserie was the name of a popular design movement in the nineteenth century, which was a Western interpretation of Chinese motifs, based on Ancient Chinese symbolism and nature. Japanese design and craft including embroidery and appliqué on garments such as kimonos, can be found in the Victoria and Albert Museum, also reflecting nature and culture. Japan is also known for rice paste and wax-resist techniques.

Indonesia. Textile crafts particularly developed around Java, and mainly comprised motifs and patterns on cotton and sometimes silk, using a wax-resist technique. The fabric was then overdyed mainly in natural red and blue dyes, indigo being popular.

Synthetic dyes later took over, and techniques with copper stamping began to be used to compete with the European market. The imagery is a mixture of Hindu, Chinese, Islamic and European influences.

Pacific Islands. Beautiful abstract and symbolic repeat patterns were traditionally made on bark cloth (the inside of tree bark) and rubbed with natural dyes and pigments. Different islands produce their own particular styles, and can also be seen in the tattoos of the islanders.

African Tribal Art. This provides a rich source of woven, embroidered, appliquéd, printed and tie and dyed resists, with each region having particular styles and fabrics. Some examples include: Fante flags from Ghana containing appliquéd symbolic

motifs, Ashanti woven clothing, dyed and stitched resists from Nigeria, Congo and Cameroon, as well as indigo using cassava starch-resist techniques, and wax resists from West Africa. Printed cloths called Kangas and Kilkois, containing symbolic imagery, were also imported to East Africa. African design and decoration was an important influence on the geometric style of patterning in Europe in the early twentieth century.

Islamic Design. The intricate geometry of patterns in architecture and the decorative arts such as ceramic tiling, can be seen as far north as southern Spain, in the former Moorish areas such as The Alhambra at Granada.

South America. Countries such as Mexico, Guatemala and Peru have a rich tradition of colourful woven and embroidered textiles. Ancient Peruvian culture also produced paintings of symbolic images using natural dyes and pigments.

Folk Art. Folk art developed in rural peasant communities throughout Eastern Europe and Scandinavia in particular, and North America, and is symbolic and naïve in style. The designs can be applied to textiles, home furnishings, toys and so on.

Twentieth-Century Design

The biggest developments in art and design took place during the twentieth century, partly due to an evolution in the fine arts, combined with huge innovations in industry and technology, and changes in society and the economy that were more rapid than at any other time in history. As a surface pattern designer it is important to be able to identify key periods, as they provide a foundation for design today. Almost each decade hailed a new development in pattern styles, imagery and colour, always reflecting the circumstances of that time and the innovations of a small number of artists and designers.

For textile design in particular, key moments during the twentieth century include the influence of abstract art that led to a break with traditional floral images in textiles during the 1930s, 1940s and 1950s. This was accelerated by the Depression of the 1930s which meant many fine artists, painters and architects in Europe and America were forced to broaden their horizons and start working in the decorative arts, in areas such as textiles and wallpaper design. Through the twentieth century, textile has also been revolutionized by the discovery of synthetic print and dye materials, and new printing methods that we use today. The past thirty years have also seen the development of fabric technology, particularly in synthetics, that has created new ways of applying pattern. Japan has been a forerunner in this development.

Print designs for fashion garments in International Textiles 1934. (Central St Martins Museum and Study Collection)

Listed below are some of the key movements and influences in surface pattern during the twentieth century.

Art Nouveau. This movement began in major European cities at the turn of the twentieth century. It crossed over from architecture into the decorative arts, and is identifiable by its curving lines, before becoming more linear through the influence of Charles Rennie Mackintosh. Art Nouveau's major influences were nature, folk art and Islamic and Asian sources.

Wiener Werkstatte. Founded in Austria by Otto Wagner, as a follow-on from the Vienna Succession at the same time as Art Nouveau. The fabrics were hand-printed for fashion and interiors, and influenced by Gustav Klimt who reflected the textiles in his paintings.

Tiffany and associated Artists. In America the late nineteenth cetury saw the beginning of Tiffany, a decorating company, and a women-only organization called the Associated Artists whose central figure was Candice Wheeler, who had an approach similar to that of William Morris in the UK (*refer* to the section on British design influences).

Bauhaus. The Bauhaus movement led by Walter Gropius has had the greatest effect on design education, and laid the foundations for the teaching of art and design today. The artists Wassail Kandinsky and Paul Klee were both teachers there, and their own work provides a great source of inspiration to surface pattern and textile designers.

Russian Constructivist Textiles. The work of designers such as Liubov Popova and Varvara Stepanova, reflected the new communist society in the USSR. The designs were functional and bold, influenced by the Russian Constructivist art movement, and reflecting scenes of agriculture, machinery and patriotic themes.

One of the most influential textile designers of the early twentieth century was Sonia Delauney, who worked with her husband Robert Delauney to develop forms of abstract colour patterning. The painter Raoul Dufy also produced many textile designs in the 1930s in collaboration with Paul Poiret, and went onto work for Bianchini-Ferrier in Lyons where over 4,000 designs were created.

Art Deco. This movement took off at the International Decorative Arts Fair in Paris in 1925. It was influenced by The Ballet Russes, which had been expelled from Russia during the Revolution, and also took its inspiration from ethnic South American design and craft, and Egyptian art. Architecture and product design reflected new ideas in streamlining which were represented in textile designs.

Mariano Fortuny. Fortuny made luxury fabrics including velvets and pleats that were ornate and elaborate, combined with technical innovations. The fabrics reflected historical styles such as the Renaissance, Byzantium and Art Nouveau. They were made for costumes, but Fortuny also worked as an interior decorator. He has a permanent museum in Venice.

The 1950s. After a lull during the War, pattern and design exploded into life, reflecting new technological developments particularly in science, and abstraction in art. Patterns were based on molecular structures or even TV aerials. This coincided with developments in synthetic fabrics and dyes. Scandinavian design was at the forefront with its more modern look, including Marimekko in Finland, and Nordiska Kampariet in Sweden.

The 1960s and 1970s. The influence of pop art and op art became influential in pattern design and textiles, colours were bright, and designs psychedelic. Design reflected exploding youth culture influenced by artists such as Andy Warhol.

The 1980s until the present. Some of the most innovative work from this period comes from Japan, particularly with the development of technology in fabric construction, including some patterning. Jun'ichi Arai was one of the main innovators, working with Issey Mayake and The Nuno Corporation.

Creation Baumann. A Swiss-based company also renowned as an innovative furnishing and interior design company. Nya Nordiska, a German company, was founded in the 1960s to produce comtemporary textile and product design.

IN BRITAIN

Arts and Crafts movement. The Victorian movement led in surface pattern by William Morris who designed and hand-produced fabrics and wallpapers. The Victoria and Albert Museum in London has an archive of work, and Kelmscott Manor, his working premises in Oxfordshire, reflect Morris's working practices. Morris and Co's designs are still in print today.

Sandersons. Founded in 1860 by Arthur Sanderson, and still in business. Sanderson initially imported luxury wallpapers from France, and also printed on behalf of Morris and Co, before producing their own design work.

Liberty and Co. As global and cultural designs began to be more accessible, particularly after the Exposition in 1862. There became a greater demand for culturally diverse products. Arthur Lasenby, aware of this growing market, opened his own shop Liberty. He could not import enough goods to satisfy demand, so resorted to designing his own fabrics in a distinctive style, designed by people such as Walter Crane and Voysey. These prints are still a hallmark and popular at Liberty today.

Omega Workshops. Short-lived design group, although its main protagonists, Duncan Grant and Vanessa Bell, continued

Wallpaper design from the1950s by Sanderson's. (Central St Martins Museum and Study Collection)

the work. Their house at Charleston in Sussex is well worth a visit to look at how surface pattern has been applied around its interiors, combined with painting and sculptural influences. **Silver Studios.** This studio was founded by Arthur Silver in the 1880s, and taken over by his son in 1900. It was the leading studio of its day producing traditional designs, some based on historical patterns found in the Victoria and Albert Museum.

Avant-garde wallpaper and textiles of that era were also produced and can be seen in a collection with other designs at Middlesex University.

Footprints and Joyce Clissold. Joyce Clissold joined the Footprints design company in 1927 and took over the company in 1933, which was established in Brentford Middlesex UK. Her design work is mainly block printed onto fabrics.

Section of a printed dress by Joyce Clissold, designer for Footprints. (Central St Martins Museum and Study Collection)

Ascher. A post-war textile company, making luxury fabrics for the fashion market, and with fashion designers such as Dior, Pierre Cardin and Elsa Schiaparelli. Some of the textiles were designed by British and French painters such as Henry Moore, Graham Sutherland and Feliks Topolski.

Artists. John Piper, Eduardo Paolozzi and Ben Nicolson all crossed over into textile pattern design in the post-war period, and the Festival of Britain in 1950 led to the development of more contemporary design. Department stores, such as Heals and Habitat in the 1960s, showcased new designers such as Lucienne Day.

Fashion designers such as Mary Quant used textile designers such as Gillian Farr, patterns were simplified and flat. Geometric patterns were also popular, such as Kinetic designs.

English Eccentrics of the 1980s and 1990s. Founded in the eighties by designer Helen Littman, who produced hand-printed designs using strong colour and images such as *trompe-l'oeil* effects. A book called *English Eccentrics* edited by Catherine McDermott gives a good insight into Helen Littman's influences and design development.

Timney Fowler. Founded in 1980, and based in London, Timney Fowler produce mainly fabrics using historical, neoclassical images for interiors.

Other influential designers include Osbourne and Little, Nigel Atkinson, and Georgina Godley.

The 1990s to the present day. Influential pattern designers include Eley Kishimoto, producing patterns for interiors and fashion, Rachel Kelly, and Timorous Beasties.

Finding a Niche for your Design Ideas

Firstly, if you are at an early stage of a potential career and would like to train seriously in textile design, you should do some research into the design courses available in your country. The UK has the biggest concentration of textile courses in the world, each offering a different approach and emphasis in art and design. If geography is not an issue, you should then look for the most relevant courses. These can range from training you to work in the commercial sector, developing your practical skills for making textiles yourself, developing new materials and technology, or even working towards fine-art textiles. If you are based in the UK, a visit to the exhibition of New Designers in London, which takes place annually in July, showcases recent graduating students' work from most of the colleges, giving you a good overview. The decision you make at this point will potentially have a huge impact on how your career develops. Even if you cannot afford a full-time commitment,

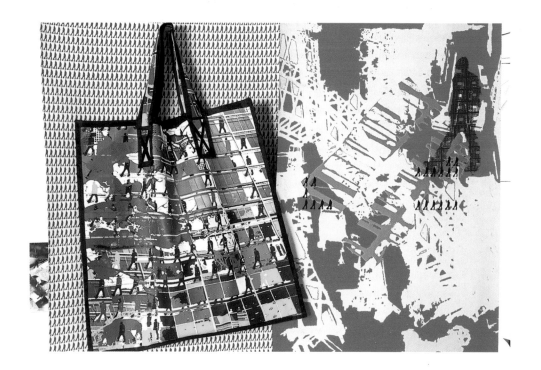

Printed wallpaper and bag design, reflecting a cityscape theme by Jessica Martin.

A commercial design printed onto a fabric garment shape, as part of a collection by Gokce Ergun for Brewster design company.

many colleges offer short introductory courses, and some formal training is essential.

By the time you have completed your training, you will have a good idea of what direction your work is going in, whether your work leans more towards the commercial industry, or you prefer making your own products, or one-off commissions. One of the exciting elements of surface pattern and textiles is that it can cross over in to different areas of the design industry, so keep your career options open while you are establishing yourself.

Three broad areas can be identified as a market or outlet for your work. These are commercial design (where only the design, or prototype of a product is necessary), designing and making your own goods, and fine-art textiles.

Commercial Designer

If you are looking to sell your work in the more commercial end of the market you may need an agent to sell your work through, if you are not working in a studio or company. Your employer or agent will give you a trend-led brief, with a theme, and a list of possible sources of inspiration, with colour and fabric direction. You will be expected to produce a co-ordinating collection of six to ten designs based on this, in either paper or fabric samples. The designs need to reflect the type of customer the company sells to, which could be menswear, womenswear, childrens wear, young and trendy, or older and sophisticated and so on. At the middle or low end of the market there will be more financial constraints, on fabrics and processes, to keep production costs down. Many designs are sold at Trade Fairs such as Indigo in Paris, Tex Print in Frankfurt and Surtex in the USA. If you are a serious freelancer, it is worth regularly visiting one of these Trade Fairs to gather information on up-and-coming trends, or to make contacts.

The box (*right*) is an example of a theme from a live brief given to students at Central St Martins College of Art and Design, by the UK-based company Brewster, who then took the designs to Paris for sale at Indigo.

THEME: **Boudoir**

▧ Lingerie story

▧ Delicate, fragile, beautiful

▧ Cut-work, embroidery

▧ Fine drawing

▧ Skin tones, make-up colours

▧ Students were asked to research these ideas, and produce twelve fashion prints on fabric showing colour development, fabrication, contrast, strong composition, exploration and presentation skills.

Designer and Maker

This is an area of design where you are more likely to work for yourself, selling more-directly to customers. This can range from one-off commissions for a client, through to orders for multiple goods in department stores or shops. As well as coming up with the idea, you will be expected to make the finished item (even if it is just one example to go into the company's production). This means more care has to be taken over permanent print or dye effects, and quality in the making of the end product that you will also need to design. As these products are generally hand-crafted, and produced in smaller numbers, they are more likely to be sold at the high end of the market, to cover costs. In the UK, trade fairs such as Chelsea Crafts Fair and 100% Design show-case this area of design.

In both commercial design and designer maker, there is a wide scope for applying surface pattern and textile design. Listed in the box (*opposite below*) are a range of products and areas you could possibly explore.

Textile Artist

If you wish to be completely free from commercial restraints, and are more interested in exploring personal ideas and experimenting with materials and processes, then you are more likely to show your work through galleries, or one-off commissions for public spaces or private clients. Magazines such as *Craft*, *American Craft* and *Artist's Newsletter* provide useful information including galleries, competitions and suppliers. The Crafts Council will also have useful contacts and information.

There are several recently published books listed in the bibliography (*see* pp.151–152), that help define the broadness of the textile industry and the possible areas of working.

Digitally printed and hand-printed aprons for a collection based on domestic textiles, by Hannah Sessions.

Lingerie collection by Tamara Boyle.

HOME INTERIORS	APPAREL	INDUSTRY	OTHERS
upholstery	womenswear	office interiors	wrapping paper
curtains/blinds	menswear	uniforms	tiles
wallpapers	childrens wear	transport (interiors)	ceramics
cushions	all clothing/coats	restaurants	giftware
tablecloths	shoes, boots	shop windows	stationery
napkins	ties		greetings cards
shower curtains	scarves		jewellery
lampshades	lingerie/tights		magazine illustration
paintings/prints	evening wear		
duvets	gloves		
bedspreads	bags		
pillows	umbrellas		
sheets	leisurewear		
rugs/carpets	sportswear		

CHAPTER 2

DESIGNING AND REPEAT PATTERNS

Once you have gathered all your research material together, experimented with drawing, painting and mark-making techniques, and have considered a possible outlet for visualizing your work, then you have all the ingredients for designing a range of finished surface patterns. This does not mean you should stop researching; it is an ongoing process. As you start designing you may find gaps in your visual information that you may need to build on, or evolve more fully for further designs.

This chapter aims to interpret your ideas into coherent and accomplished surface patterns, by introducing a set of important design principles that will help structure your images, colour and texture, in a visually exciting way.

Before you start, it is worth making a few points about the visual material you intend to use. Unless you are working towards fine-art textiles, or don't wish to sell your work commercially, your designs will need to take into account what is suitable for your market. If you are working towards the mainstream market, you will need to avoid using any controversial imagery, for example, images with religious or political overtones. Also take into account any limitations on materials and production costs, for example, the colour range for production may be limited to only four colours. Work closely with your agent or company to find out what exactly their market is, and continually ask for feedback. If you are making your own products don't overburden yourself with over-elaboration that is time consuming and expensive to make.

'Dolls' wallpaper design in a conversational style, by Donald Melbourne for Shand Kydd Focus. (By kind permission of CWV Group Ltd)

Influential Design Themes

The commercial sector relies on a few general and long-established themes that are always the stable part of the surface pattern design market, and will continually come in and out of fashion (*see* Chapter 1).

Florals

Floral and botanical images have always taken up the biggest part of the surface pattern design market. Through history there has always been a tradition of reflecting nature in design, representing the beauty of the natural world around us, and being symbolic and representative of national identity. The textile industry is also more female-led, and florals are more representative of femininity. The scope for interpreting flora and fauna into design is enormous, with a huge variety of colour, shapes and textures available, applicable to any mood and season.

Geometrics

Another huge part of the surface pattern design market historically, is geometric design. Such designs have been sourced from both the man-made and natural world, crossing over both the male and female markets. Although geometrics can be 'loud' and bright, they can also provide unchallenging, inoffensive patterns, suitable for every taste. A small selection of geometric pattern ideas include blocks, cubes, plaids, grids, concentric circles, diamond shapes, tile patterns, ogee shapes, herringbone, swirls, polka dots and optical art.

Floral design by June Fish.

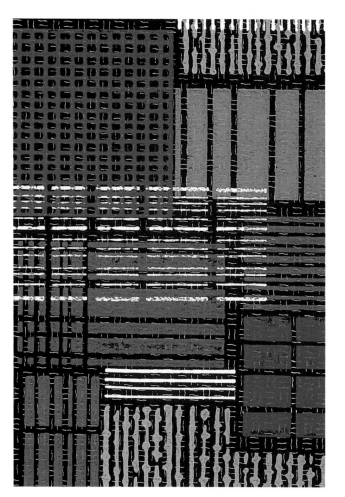

LEFT: **'Barra', geometric wallpaper design by Donald Melbourne for Shand Kydd Focus. (By kind permission of CWV Group Ltd)**

Ethnic

Ethnic design and tribal art from around the world is also pop-ular as a theme, and is often a major trend forecasted. Ethnic design offers an alternative way of representing the other major themes such as florals and geometrics, particularly in the use of materials and processes, such as batik and embroidery. The ethnic theme can extend across all national cultures including European folk arts and crafts, to African tribal costume, body adornment and jewellery (*see* Chapter 1).

Conversationals

Conversationals represent a style of design that is more graph-ic, with greater visual impact. Historically, themes included interpretations of people and their day-to-day life, including work and leisure activities, also known as genre painting. Also categorized are mythological scenes, landscape and animals, and cityscapes and architecture. Conversationals can be as detailed as just using animal fur, feathers and camouflage in nature, for overall patterns. Objects are also another main source of inspiration, including toys, jewellery, instruments, homeware, food and machinery. Writing and numbers would also come under this grouping. Traditionally, these would have been painted, but now include photographic and computer-generated imagery.

Non-Print Prints

This term is used to describe patterns that don't actually constitute any type of imagery, but are just made from textures or mark-making. This can involve brushwork, stippling and embossing. These types of print are particularly useful in interiors, where they appear understated and an unchallenging backdrop to furnishings.

Although each area has been separately categorized above, they often cross over; a non-print print may provide a backdrop for a conversational, or a floral could be combined with a geometric. The combinations are endless and the turnover of ideas is quick, so a good variety of available source material from all areas is essential.

You should now interpret your resource material with your 'own hand', that is to say redrawn, repainted or reassembled with your own style and imagination. Although you may take inspiration from the work of others, it is important not to copy it directly as you may be breaking laws on copyright. Later on in the chapter we will look more closely at this matter, as you may also need to protect your own design work from being plagiarized.

Listed below are the different design components you will need to consider using together in an innovative and coherent way if you are to produce a range of successful designs:

▦ Concept/Imagery
▦ Style of working
▦ Scale
▦ Texture
▦ Composition
▦ Pattern
▦ Colour.

All the components will need to interact together before you can achieve a successful outcome. You will probably have to try several combinations and variations, such as different colour ways or changing the scale of the imagery, before it all clicks, and you have found your finished design.

Concept/Imagery

The concept is the theme, mood or inspiration behind the design (see Chapter 1). This may be from a set brief from forecasted trends in fashion or interiors, or a personal brief if you are working more independently. An example of a concept for a project is a self-directed student brief by Frederique Denniel, for her final Degree Collection called 'Poubelles Poetiques'.

The aim of the project is to make a collection of original fabrics that reveal the beauty, poetry and diversity of shapes, colours and textures of London's rubbish. The designs are developed from photographs, painted collages to source colour and texture, and heat set to capture the 3D shapes of the thrown-away objects. (Chapter 4 shows the results of her work.)

Inspiration is taken from the work of Issey Miyake, John Galliano and Yohji Yamamoto, and the market aimed for is textile furnishings.

The work will be presented through an exhibition and photographic portfolio presentation.

Your concept will need to include ideas for imagery or motifs, colour, pattern and composition, fabric, and end function. A good way to initially put these different ideas together is to create a mood board, representing a snapshot of all the elements from your concept. This is an A2-sized board collaged together with samples of drawing, fabric, photos, writing and so on (see Chapter 3 on presentation). This will provide a general overall picture to show a client, or just clarify ideas for yourself.

Often commercial briefs combine a mixture of different inspirational sources under one theme or concept, so don't feel restricted. Below is a brief produced by the design company Brewster for Indigo in Paris, containing several ideas under one heading:

Global Traveller

▦ African mixed with Victorian
▦ Eclectic mixes of influences
▦ Tribal mixed with traditional
▦ Embroidery
▦ Damask
▦ Indian prints over Liberty prints
▦ Found fabrics
▦ 1970s in feel
▦ Stripes mixed with ethnics.

THIS PAGE:
Mood board showing visual ideas reflecting the theme 'Comfort Zone', by Aya Tsukai.

OPPOSITE PAGE:
A design for Brewster's 'Global Traveller' theme, by Gokce Ergun.

Style

Your experiments with different drawing and painting media (*see* Chapter 1) will now be extremely useful, to enable you to find the most suitable way of interpreting your ideas. For example, if your theme is city architecture, then a graphic, linear style may be more relevant, using neutral colours; or a natural theme such as summer florals could be extremely painterly in bright textured colours.

You will need to think about the overall look and feel of the design. For example, do you want the design to look static and organized, or more chaotic with a feeling of movement? The design could be packed with overlapping busy imagery, or be spacious and calm. Does the imagery in the design need to create the illusion of looking solid or 3D, requiring depth and shading in your drawing methods, or is it flat and 2D, where collage might do to create the effect? Again, remember your design could be a mixture of these things, the background could be painterly with flowing movement, and static images could be drawn on top. This again may take a few tries and different combinations to work out, in relation to the other design principles overleaf.

Busy and vibrant repeat patterns for a ladieswear collection, by Bianca Ward.

Texture

Texture is particularly important for textile designers, as the weight and surface texture of a paper or fabric can really add to the mood and feel of a design. The type of material you use should correspond with your theme, or intended market; for example, if your design theme is based on a richly coloured, decadent look, then a velvet or heavy silk will provide tactility to add to the mood (*see* Chapters 3 and 6 for textured paper and fabric types).

The uneven layering of ink, stitching, gluing, bonding, or burning and cutting back into fabric, all enhance textured surfaces.

Purely visual texture that has little impact on the surface quality of the fabric is another avenue to explore. Painted and printed marks and dye processes can create the illusions of texture (*see* Chapter 3 for information on processes).

Composition and Layout

The composition of your design involves the organization of all your design material into a coherent and balanced layout. The space in between patterns or motifs needs to be considered, so that there are no awkward blank areas. Before tackling colour it is worth sketching out or collaging your design in black and white (multiple photocopies are useful) to check that the design is evenly distributed and consistent. Make sure there are no awkward gaps, or overworked unreadable areas. Textile designs do not have to fit within the borders of the paper, and imagery should be seen to be coming off the edge, to give an indication of how it will continue in repeat, which we will look at later in this chapter.

Pattern Structures

There are a range of well recognized pattern structures that you will continually use. As mentioned in Chapter 1, if you are

Scale

The scale or size of the imagery is particularly important in relation to an end product. Surface patterns on fashion garments will tend to be smaller than those on a furnishing print due to the amount of surface area they are covering, although this can sometimes vary. The design on the pattern could be smaller in scale to have less impact than large bold images if perhaps it is for wallpaper, or will be smaller if it is an all-over design, rather than a one-off placing of a motif. There are no rules set in stone though, and a design could easily be a combination of different-size motifs and patterns.

producing designs for the fashion or furnishing markets it is quite often expected that you produce a collection or group of designs that are variations of one theme, and are co-ordinating. Using established structures will give you lots of options to show your initial design ideas in a variety of ways. Also, if you are unsure how to begin formatting your imagery, then using the pattern frameworks listed below will help you overcome this problem. It can be daunting, particularly if you are designing a large-scale repeated design that can be hard to visualize, so applying a proven formula is useful.

Stripes. Stripes are a standard form of patterning that never goes out of fashion; they can originate from man-made or natural structures. The stripes themselves may contain rows of images, of varying widths and dimensions, and can also develop into plaids, grids, cheques and tartans. Stripes can be irregularly spaced, they may be in diagonals or undulating. Often in design, stripes are used as a background pattern or for a co-ordinating design and can be worked on top of.

Borders. Border designs can be used as edging around fashion garments and furnishings, helping to create a finish to the design, or more practically to allow for a stronger edge to stop fabrics fraying and wearing out. A border also allows for a break in the design so that different colours or design motifs can be used. Often wallpapers will have a border around the middle, with either side of the border being different, or if the design is understated, a border can be a small injection of vibrant colour and imagery.

Squares. Creating boxes for your motifs to sit in, is an easy way of putting different images together comfortably, and creates a

Design for a striped co-ordinate, by Aya Tsukai.

Design placed in uniform boxes, by Aya Tsukai.

31

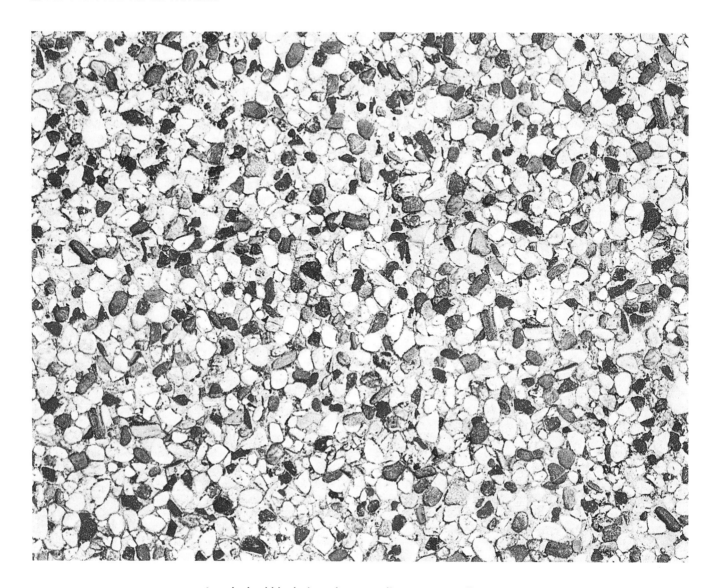

A packed pebble design, almost reading as an overall texture,
by Crown Wallpapers. (By kind permission of CWV Group Ltd)

patchwork of pattern. The boxes can be uniform or irregular in shape, and of different sizes, which helps overcome the problem of images that look awkward together without any framework. **Single and multiple images.** A surface pattern may be made up of just one singular image repeated all over the design in a repeat format. Single images that are repeated like this may be used to create an overall texture or background pattern. Small motifs used in this way are sometimes called *ditsies*. A design may also be made up of multiple images, which can be joined together or spaced out separately, combining together to work as an overall pattern structure. Some designs are referred to as '*packed*', which is when there are so many images crammed into the design that it almost reads as an overall texture.

OPPOSITE PAGE:
Straight repeat of teacake motifs, by Hannah Sessions.

Straight repeat design.

Brick repeat design.

Half-drop design.

Vertical and horizontal
mirror image design.

Vertical mirror
image design.

All-over pattern design.

Stripe design in a
diagonal format.

Example of a
border design.

An irregularly
spaced design.

Single and multi-directionals. The motifs in your pattern can also be positioned in different directions. Single directional images are where the images are seen as being upright; and two-directional images are usually upright and upside down. Images can also be multi-directional, and scattered in all directions, and the design may have no readable right way up. This can also create an impression of movement in the design. Multi-directional designs are useful particularly on printed lengths that are to be made into garments, as the fabric patterns can be cut anywhere, which enables you to cut across the bias of the fabric if you are making accessories such as ties.

Repeat Structures

A repeat design takes your pattern structure a stage further and indicates how a design would work if it was put into production, and was repeated over and over again on a length of fabric. The repeat should work without any awkward joins visible, so that the design flows easily and seamlessly across the fabric.

If you are working freelance for the fashion industry it is not expected that you should always put everything into an accurate repeat to sell a design, as long as you can suggest how it repeats. In furnishing design, it is more likely that you would be expected to show an accurate repeat, as the fabric pieces needed are much greater in scale.

You may need to print repeat lengths of fabric yourself if you are selling your own fabrics directly to customers, so it is important to learn how to do this properly, but without letting it stifle the creativity of your work. If you find it difficult to visualize your work in repeat, then there are computer programs such as Photoshop specific to this task that can translate your designs into different repeat formats in an instant.

A range of established set of repeat formats includes:

straight repeat: where the image or motif forms straight horizontal and vertical lines.
half drop: the vertical lines of images are dropped halfway between the images on either side.
brick repeat: the horizontal line images are moved halfway between images on either side.
mirrored image: where your images are mirror reflections of themselves horizontally or vertically, or both at the same time.
ogee: this is a half drop, where the image also fits into a different shape, which is onion-shaped in appearance.

Putting a Design into Repeat

These formats will automatically put motifs of a similar size into repeat, but if your images are of varying sizes and you wish to position them more freely in the design, you will have to work out your own repeat format. Computer programs such as Photoshop will do this for you, or the repeat pattern can be worked out by hand. Start off by photocopying your design (making sure the design doesn't get distorted by the photocopier), as you will need to cut through it. At each stage you will need to re-photocopy the design so that it can be cut and pasted together. Having a few spare photocopies of the design is useful as it will give you a general overview of what it looks like repeated, when they are placed together, before you commit yourself to a final repeat.

A design combining a background repeat pattern overprinted with a singular image, by Natalie Hand.

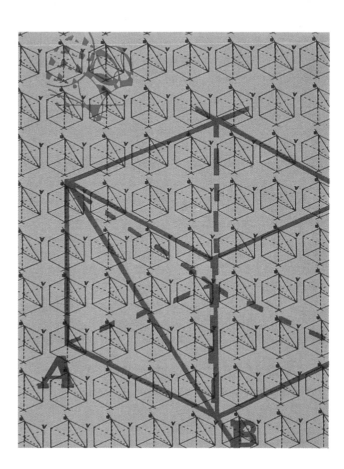

You will need a:

- Light box
  (or some type of light source – a window will do)
- Clear plastic grid
- Pencil
- Scalpel
- Ruler
- Scissors
- Masking tape and Sellotape.

It is important to be as accurate as possible, so make sure that you use your light box and grid under the design to keep it straight, and that your scalpel and pencil are as sharp as possible, as any woolly lines can create a gap or overlap in the repeat.

Firstly, you will need to place and gently attach your design to the grid, and draw four small crosses in each corner of the design, using the same grid lines to keep them in line with each other. These crosses will prove invaluable when repeating the design accurately. Then draw a line through the centre of your design from top to bottom; this does not need to be a straight line. Find a route through that avoids drawing directly into the middle of motifs or patterns, but only goes around the edges of them – it doesn't matter how wavy the line is (see Fig. a).

Cut the design in half, along the drawn line, and then swop over both sides, so the outer edges of the design are now in the middle. Make sure that the drawn crosses remain on the same grid lines, so that the design remains straight (see Fig. b).

You have now created a side-to-side repeat that will print the length of your paper or fabric over and over again, but you will need to recompose the middle section of the design before you can go ahead and repeat the design in the other direction. This is to fill in gaps that have now been created, or images that are now overlapping each other, and may need removing.

Once you have resolved the middle section, then rephotocopy your new design. This time draw a line horizontally through the centre of the design from one side to the other, avoiding the images (see Fig. c).

Cut through again, and swop the top and bottom sections of the design over, carefully repositioning the design on the grid using your crosses to keep the design straight. Again recompose the middle section of the design (see Fig. d).

Now that your design repeats in both directions, you may wish to photocopy it a few times to visually see the repeat, particularly if you need to show it accurately in your finished design. The images can be traced over, and transferred onto paper so that your layout is exact.

OPPOSITE PAGE:

TOP LEFT: **Making a repeat design. Cut through the centre of your design, avoiding images if possible, and swop over the two halves of the design, so that the left side is now on the right.**

TOP RIGHT: **Reorganize the layout of the centre of your design. The dark areas represent new images drawn in to fill in awkward gaps created.**

BOTTOM LEFT: **Cut through your design horizontally, avoiding images, and swop both halves over.**

BOTTOM RIGHT: **Again fill in any awkward gaps. Your design now repeats from left to right, and top to bottom.**

If you are intending to transfer the image to silk screen for repeat printing onto fabric or wallpaper, then you will need to extend the repeat in one direction to cover the width of your fabric or wallpaper. Decide which way you want the images to print on the fabric or paper, before extending the repeat. Use your grid to redraw some accurate crosses in the corners of the design, as this will help you line it up accurately for exposure onto the screen. Then carefully Sellotape a few of the finished copies of the repeat together accurately, again using your crosses to line up each repeat. A specialist photocopy shop will be able to then rephotocopy the whole repeat on one large sheet of paper if the stuck together pieces are proving too flimsy, as you will continually need to use them when lining up your silk screens. This only provides a one-colour print, and if you are using multiple colours, each image colour will need to be separated out onto different sheets of paper, or repainted onto drafting film, for each colour screen (see Chapter 7).

Colour and Chromafile (by Garth Lewis)

Colour is often the most important component of a design, and many people are attracted to products, paintings and textiles, because of the colour palette. Colour is both perceptual and symbolic, reflecting feelings, atmosphere, information, social function and status, as well as having direct appeal to our senses. The significance and power of colour cannot be underestimated, and whether for designing or marketing products, there is a continuous need to reappraise and reinvent colour

a.

b.

c.

d.

**Colour co-ordinates for a design
collection by Gokce Ergun.**

ranges. Textile designers may have to create their own colours or work within specified colour palettes that are predicted for seasons: autumn/winter, spring/summer; colour forecasting can be a career in itself.

Throughout history, textiles has been an arena for the development of new colours, for the recognition and understanding of colour and for its practical use in dying, constructing or printing fabrics. For a designer the interplay, grouping and mixing of colours is critical, whether producing 'colourways' (alternative colour palettes for a single design), colour matching designs to printed fabric or dyed yarns, or in the creation of new textiles.

The use of virtual colour with computer aided-design and manufacture has greatly increased the number and type of colours a designer can use. The average viewer can distinguish about one hundred thousand colours, but computers offer new systems that produce millions of colours.

The ability to mix colours and create dynamic or harmonious colour relationships, is achieved through practise and a certain amount of trial and error; however, some knowledge and understanding of colour principles and colour language can assist the designer's colour experiments and colour expression. The illustrations on pp. 39–42 show terms and ideas used in reference to paint and material colour.

About Colour

Terms and ideas commonly used in reference to paint colour:

Colour (also Hue)

A quality of visible phenomena distinct from form, light and shade.

Hue

That attribute to which colours may be described as red, yellow, blue, green, etc. Red-orange denotes a hue equally resembling red and orange.

Value

The attribute that measures variation among greys; refers to the lightness and darkness of a colour.

Any hue can vary in value. For example, red can become light pink or dark maroon.

Normal Value

Value most characteristic of each colour. Usually, the value of paint right out of the tube.

Shade

Below the normal value.
Maroon is a shade of red that has a lower value.

Tint

Above the normal value. Pink is a tint of red that has a higher value.

Chroma

The quality that embraces hue and saturation together.

Chromatic

Reds, greens, purples, browns, pinks and so on.

Achromatic
Without chroma: black, white, greys.

Saturation
That attribute to which colours may be seen as higher or lower in degrees of vividness.
Fully saturated: pure colour with the least admixture.
Desaturated: losing purity of colour, becoming less chromatic.

Colour Wheel
A systemic mixing guide showing a sequence of colours in an orderly progression.

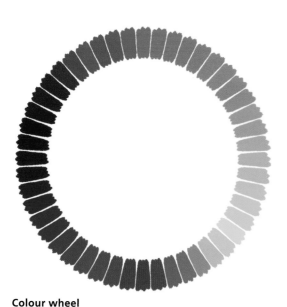

Colour wheel

Beginning with:

Primary Colours
Red, yellow and blue. Cannot be mixed from other colours.

Secondary Colours
Orange, green and violet. Colours that can be mixed from primary colours.
Yellow and red make orange, for example.

Tertiary Colours
Combinations of primary and secondary colours: yellow-green, blue-violet, red-orange and so on.

Analogous Colours
Those colours with a common hue that are adjacent on the colour wheel, for example blue-violet, violet and red-violet.

Complementary Colours

Those which oppose optically; colours represented opposite each other on the colour wheel, such as red-green, blue-orange, yellow-violet.

Subtractive Colour

Pigment and paint colour mixing: red, yellow and blue in combination produces a neutral grey-black.

Colour Scheme

Any plan using colour with some limitations.

Monochromatic

A colour scheme using (variations of) one hue.

Vibrating Colour

When complementary colours of equal value are placed together, they cause a visual intensity exceeding their actual intensity. This is also known as Simultaneous Contrast.

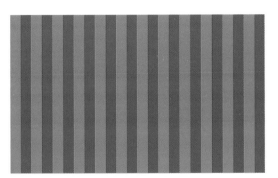

Simultaneous Contrast

Characterizes colour as a strongly relative phenomenon; colours change their appearance depending on their context.

In any colour scheme, as important as the identity of a particular colour is the relationship it shares with the other colours in the composition. An individual colour can change its identity in many ways: a dull colour can be brightened, a strong colour subdued, depending on the colours with which it is surrounded.

Simultaneous contrast is demonstrated when complementary colours are placed together – at their shared edge, they each appear more intense. Red appears redder, and the green, greener. This demonstrates simultaneous contrast of colour: their difference is emphasized.

A: When two colours are placed together, there will be an interaction and each will be enhanced or diminished. In some cases there will be a hue change.

B: When a mid-grey is placed on lighter and darker greys there will be a Value change.
On the lighter ground the mid-grey will appear darker, on the darker ground it will appear lighter.

Copyright Issues

Issues surrounding copyright and plagiarism have been difficult to establish in fashion and textiles, more so than other design disciplines. This is because commercial fashion and textiles is more affected by trends, and cycles involving certain themes; colour schemes and styles that most designers will be expected to adhere to. There is no doubt that freelance designers are in a vulnerable position as far as protecting their work from copying, and if working in the commercial area of textiles you may accept this as part of the norm.

Despite this, guidelines have been set up to offer some protection, under the 1988 Act for Surface Pattern. As a designer you should always sign and date your work, and keep either a photographic record or a small cut-off piece of the design. This offers immediate copyright protection for twenty-five years. If you are passing your work on to an agent to sell on your behalf you should check their arrangements and procedures in place to protect your design work, particularly for exhibitions, and when showing their clients. If you are sending your work in for competitions, then it is your responsibility to protect your work, but check with the promoter what the implications will be if you win, whether you are entitled to royalties or if you have to hand over production rights. Make sure that even if you do not win, the promoter returns your work and does not use any of your ideas.

The law states that a design can be influenced by someone else's idea, but must be redesigned completely, to produce an alternative, and not a copy. A differentiation between a design and an idea needs to be made, to avoid any infringement. If you are producing your own work without having to follow established trends in industry, then copyright and plagiarism issues can have much more serious repercussions. The Chartered Society of Designers offers support and advice, so it may be worth joining, particularly if you are working as a sole trader or small company. Other organizations include the Fashion Design Protection Association. Another organization frequently used by designers is called ACID (Anti Copying in Design). This organization offers support and legal advice on design protection, and once a member you can use the company's logo alongside your work to act as a deterrent.

This can also work in reverse and you need to make sure that you do not infringe others' work, even if it is subconsciously done. Completely avoid using any logos, symbols and established corporate images from companies or other designers, unless you ask and receive permission. All these images will have been copyrighted and you are breaking the law if you use them.

Not all images and motifs come under copyright laws, particularly older ones. The Dover bookshop produces a range of books with images and motifs that can be freely used, as they are no longer copyrighted, so it is worth finding your local supplier; there is also a website from which you can order books.

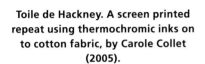

Toile de Hackney. A screen printed repeat using thermochromic inks on to cotton fabric, by Carole Collet (2005).

CHAPTER 3

WORKING FROM
PAPER ONTO FABRIC

This chapter aims to take the practical work done on paper, in Chapters 1 and 2, a stage further, to begin the transition of applying your patterning ideas onto fabric. This is to enable similar methods and ideas to be easily transferred from one to another, without the outcome altering too much. Alternative methods of working will be shown where paper methods are not suitable on fabric but similar results need to be achieved on fabric, and vice versa.

Most designers feel more confident and in control of the materials they are using on paper, and there can sometimes be a 'fear' of moving onto fabric, as inexperienced designers and makers have less knowledge of fabric dyes, inks and adhesives. The work can end up less developed and experimental on fabric, because mistakes may be more costly on expensive materials. Sometimes the ingenuity and spontaneity of paperwork design is therefore lost, and the surface pattern on fabric is stifled and rigid, and loses the designer's creativeness and personal signature. This chapter will show that this need not happen. Also make sure that you are familiar with pattern structures, so are confident and direct about the way you apply the materials.

Many textile fabric inks, dyes and equipment can also be used on paper, so can add depth to your paperwork. Where possible, this chapter hopes to break down the barriers and make techniques interchangeable between paper and fabric.

If you have done little printing or painting onto fabric, it is a good idea to work out your initial prints on paper before committing yourself to fabrics, as you will also need to check that your silk screen and ink is printing properly. Fabric requires more chemicals and finishing processes if the pattern needs to be applied permanently, so you will not want to get into this at an early stage. Once you feel more confident then you can start introducing fabric samples alongside your paperwork ideas. Try not to be too conscious of making mistakes, as both paper and fabric designs can easily be overprinted or painted, or cut up and intercut, collaged or stitched, combining different sections of your designs, until you are happy with the final result. If you can access a computer and scanner (see Chapter 4) then scanning unfinished designs will give you the opportunity to try out alternative formats and colours.

If you have no experience of using fabric inks and dyes, it is worth spending a day or so producing some technical and colour fabric swatches, to get a feel for mixing colour and fabric texture. Refer to the recipes in Chapters 6 and 7 to develop an understanding of what is involved, so you can manipulate the processes to obtain results more applicable to your ideas. If you are working in a small studio at home, you may have to find ways of altering or compromising methods if you cannot access certain equipment or chemicals.

For freelance designers it is important to note that many textile agents and companies now require designs to be produced on fabric samples instead of paper. This enables companies to give a better indication of the feel and handle of the fabric, as an extra selling point. This does not necessarily mean that the fabric needs to be finished to a high standard, and the overall treatment and fixation of the fabric is not crucial as you are only selling the idea, which gives more scope for using a wider variety of materials on fabric.

Block-printed and devoré printed dress on a sumptuous velvet fabric, by Joyce Clissold. (Central St Martins Museum and Study Collection)

45

Types of Paper and Fabric

Paper

It is important to work on good quality papers that willl not weaken and cockle under the amount of dye, paint and ink you may apply to them, as this will look unprofessional. You do not need to necessarily work from white paper, as textured or pre-coloured papers may enhance and complement your design work. Brown wrapping paper is interesting to work on, and inexpensive.

It is also a good idea to try and relate the type of paper you are using to the type of fabric you intend to end up printing on. For instance, if you are planning to print onto a raw textured silk, then silk paper or textured papers might reflect that more and give you a better idea of how the finished design may look before you commit yourself to fabric. If you are testing out some patterning techniques, wallpaper lining paper is useful as it doesn't warp when printed and, if you need to practise a large patterned repeat, it is inexpensive to use on a large scale.

Cartridge Paper. If you are at the beginning of the designing process then white cartridge paper is a good starting place, as it is inexpensive and yields good results. Cartridge paper is also good for collaging or intercutting into other designs, as it is flat and untextured. Try to use a thicker weight of cartridge

Printing onto a textured wood-dust paper.

Stretching paper.

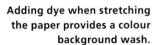

Adding dye when stretching the paper provides a colour background wash.

paper (130–150g are good weights to use) particularly if you are planning to apply dye and paint. Even so, you will probably need to stretch the paper on a drawing board to avoid it cockling. **Watercolour Paper.** If you want to avoid stretching the paper then you will probably need to use a heavier paper such as watercolour paper that soaks up paint and dye without cockling. Some watercolour papers have interesting textures, which can also add to your design. They will be more expensive to

use, so it is worth waiting until you have experimented with your ideas on cartridge paper. Most papers are cotton based, and the weights of paper are usually between 190 and 300g.

Different types of paper include:

■ Cotman – an inexpensive, grainy paper and a good alternative to cartridge and expensive watercolour papers;

- Bockingford – economical paper, with an interesting texture, caused by the pressure applied by woollen blankets in a cylinder mould machine;
- Somerset – inexpensive quality paper;
- Saunders Waterford – stable and durable paper;
- Fabriano – easy to work on, durable;
- Aquarelle – extremely high quality paper;
- Royal Water Colour Society Paper – high quality mixture of cotton and linen.

Silk papers are highly textured, sometimes delicate, almost translucent papers, with strands and fibres of silk embedded in the structure.

Tracing paper and drafting film can help re-create the effects of sheer translucent fabrics such as georgette, although paint effects may chip off if applied too thickly.

Chromulux papers have a plastic laminated surface, are opaque and come in a variety of colours.

Recycled and handmade papers: handmade papers can be embedded with florals, leaves and other plant fibres, to create interesting textures and colours. These can be purchased in specialist paper shops or, if you have the time, you can attempt to make them yourself, particularly if you have access to a press. Photocopy paper is best to use for the pulp as it is cheap and stable, and any vegetable skins and flora and fauna can be used to give the paper a unique organic look.

Patterned papers: it is also possible to buy already printed or marbled papers, that you may find interesting to overprint, collage or pattern into a new design. Be careful to only use basic images such as animal prints, as you may be infringing another designer's work. This is useful and complementary if you are also intending to work on recycled or second-hand fabrics that also have simple patterns already on them. You will probably need to use a range of opaque inks, that will overprint on top clearly, as standard inks will sink in and disappear into already coloured papers.

Fabric

It is incredibly important to use fabrics suitable for the type of textiles you are making, particularly taking into account the possible end function of your work. A distinction between furnishing and fashion fabrics is the most obvious difference. Using fabric that is suitable for the particular dyeing, painting and printing processes that you are using needs to be planned ahead. Your fabric should enhance the mood and theme of your design work. If you are at the experimental stages it is probably worth buying a small quantity of a variety of fabrics, to try out techniques and fabric textures. Most shops or market stalls will sell half metres or one-metre lengths. Make sure the supplier is clear about what they are selling you – that it is *not* a synthetic equivalent of a silk or wool (*see* Chapter 5 for information on fibre identification).

FASHION AND FURNISHING FABRICS

Fabrics are generally divided into these two types, although this does not include performance and outdoor fabrics. These categorizations do cross over, and some fabrics can be multi-purpose.

If you are thinking of applying your surface pattern ideas to inner garments or scarves, it is important to buy fabrics that are comfortable to wear and drape well. Fashion fabrics usually come in a smaller width than furnishing fabrics and will contain a good selection of sheer and lightweight fabrics that would be totally unsuitable for most furnishing uses as they would not be durable enough. Hard-wearing fabrics good for interiors could also be suitable for outer fashion garments. Some harder-wearing fabrics can be waterproofed and used for outdoor purposes. Fabrics for fashion wear are seasonal, lighter weights are used more in spring/summer, and heavier wools and cottons in winter. Listed in the box (*opposite*) is a range of fabric types from light- to heavy-weight styles.

FABRICS WITH PAPER QUALITIES

Some non-woven fabrics can almost have a paper-like look and feel, if you are keen to carry this look on from your paperwork. Tyvek is one such fabric. It is versatile in its use, and can still be used to make functional textiles. Some nylon fabrics can also have a similar feel and texture to fabric, paper nylon being a specific type.

Applying Print/Pattern Processes to Paper and Fabric

Before starting, try to gather as many different painting and printing tools and equipment as possible to be able to experiment more freely with a variety of pattern and mark-making techniques. The more you have at your disposal the more exciting and progressive the results will be. If you are on a tight budget it does not necessarily mean you have to spend a fortune

A SELECTION OF LIGHT-, MEDIUM- AND HEAVYWEIGHT FABRICS

Lightweight fabrics include:

- Organza: this is a sheer, stiff fabric, and can be made from different fibres including silk and polyester

- Organdie: sheer cotton equivalent

- Crepe: a partially sheer, softer textured fabric

- Chiffon: delicate fabric

- Habotai: a range of shiny silk fabrics, ideal for fashion

- Lawn: light cotton fabric

- Muslin: loosely woven cotton

Medium-weight fabrics include:

- Twill: diagonal textured cotton

- Duck: hard-wearing cotton fabric

- Poplin: plain weave

- Taffeta: shiny fabric in silk and polyester

- Sateen: shiny fabric

Heavier-weight fabrics include:

- Drill: hard-wearing cotton

- Denim: hard-wearing cotton

- Furnishing satin: shiny, smooth fabric

- Corduroy: ridged fabric for both fashion and furnishing

- Velvet: piled fabric in cotton, silk and polyester, good for fashion and interiors

- Canvas: a tough cotton, ideal for paintings, backdrops and, if treated, an outdoor material

- Felt: a chunky, absorbent, textured fabric, usually wool or can be synthetic. A good insulating fabric so is useful in a winter collection
  (If you have time you can felt your own wool, which would be complementary and a possible follow-on from making your own paper. Felt can also be moulded into 3D shapes. A specialist felt-making book is worth looking at if you are interested in exploring this further.)

All the fabrics above do come in different weights and fibre types, so only use this as a general guide. There are many more hybrids and fibre mixtures, with special qualities such as stretch, waterproofing and so on.

Upholstered chair made from hard-wearing wool, and hand-printed in acid dye, by Ahreum Han.

in an art and craft shop. A visit to a hardware shop or even your own garage or kitchen may yield some useful brushes or textured surfaces. A toothbrush can be as effective as a spray diffuser. The materials listed below cover the techniques listed in this chapter.

Materials

- A good selection of paintbrushes with different widths (household brushes are useful)
- Hard bristle brushes; a nailbrush, toothbrush or scrubbing brush would work
- Sponges
- Spray, such as garden spray container, or spray diffuser
- Scalpel and metal ruler
- Pencils
- Ink pens
- Wooden drawing board
- Newsprint or newspaper
- Silk screen
- Squeegee
- Plastic pots and paints palette
- Spoons and wooden stirrers
- Perspex or sheet of acetate
- Ink roller
- Masking tape, clear tape
- Fabric rags
- Iron, heat press
- Sewing machine, needles, thread and pins

Silk-Screen Methods

Many of the techniques described in this chapter require the use of a silk screen. Printing through a silk screen enables inks and dyes to be distributed evenly and in a controlled manner onto paper or fabric, which is difficult to achieve particularly when working directly onto fabric. A sample silk screen about 700mm x 500mm in diameter (around A2 size) is suitable for producing work on saleable sample sizes, and also makes it convenient to work on a small table space. You may use the screen in a blank format, working directly on the clear screen mesh, or using resist fillers to block out certain areas. At some point it may be necessary for you to have your images exposed directly onto the screen, which is a chemical method of transferring detailed

images semi-permanently. Once on screen the images can be reused countless times, so it is particularly useful for large numbers of repeat prints, and if you need intricate prints such as writing or linear images, which can't be done easily by stencil. The section on setting up a silk screen in Chapter 7 will explain this process further, but look through this section first to see what can be achieved without chemical exposure, as it may be difficult to find the necessary facilities to carry out this process. There are home-made ways of screen exposure, but the results are unpredictable, as it also relies on ultraviolet light. It may be good to source out a local college or print workshop that will hire out the facilities necessary for exposing and cleaning your screens.

A good quality squeegee is also necessary (see Chapter 7 for materials and techniques for screen printing).

Silk-Screen Printing with Semi-Permanent Images

If you have been able to have your silk screen coated with light-sensitive emulsion and exposed with ultraviolet light so that your images are semi-permanent, then use the screen to its full capacity. That is to say by finding as many different combinations of compositions, colours and overprints with the imagery as possible. If it is for sample designs and not a repeat print, pack as many singular images on the screen leaving a slight border around the edges, so that you have room to put a layer of gum strip to stop ink getting stuck in the gap between mesh and frame. Once on the screen you can print the motifs separately by covering the other images up with paper when you are printing.

A sample screen can be used multi-directionally, and one image can be printed countless times before the ink dries in to the mesh. If you have space on your table for several fabric and paper samples, then work on a few at the same time by planning out a sequence of printing. Try and avoid overprinting on a wet print that will stick to the back of the screen and be reprinted as a shadow print elsewhere.

Fabric printing inks will be sufficient on paper, preferably stretched on a board. If you need a high quality print on paper it may be worth switching to an acrylic-based medium with extender, for going through the silk screen, which will also work well on a heavy cotton canvas.

Remember to be experimental and combine and overprint different motifs together. Always start printing with the lightest colour first, and build up to darker colours, so that you can always overprint.

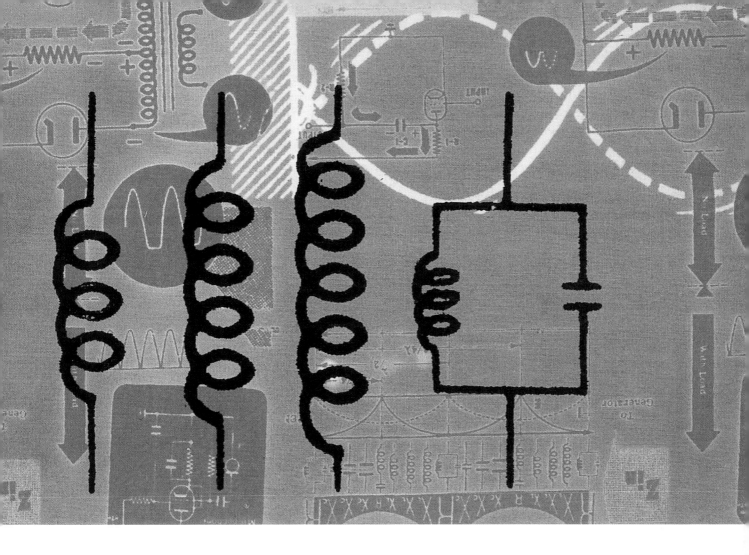

Fabric sample over-printed with screen stencil images several times to build up layers of pattern, by June Fish.

If you do want to produce screened images, and proper screen exposure of images is not possible, then there are alternatives such as paper stencils and screen fillers and fluids. Methods for these are included in the following pages. If you do need to produce a large number of the same prints, it is recommended that you find a way to have your screens properly exposed, as the screen filler methods do break down quickly.

Screen Filler and Drawing Fluids

Screen filler is a water-based substance that can be painted onto the screen to block out any areas that you do not wish to be printed. The liquid may have to be dried overnight before being used. Once dried, the screen filler will provide a barrier while you are printing ink through the remaining clear screen area onto your paper or fabric. The screen filler can then be washed off with an appropriate cleaner or even with household bleach. The method above only really allows for quite bold shapes and textured marks. If you need it to be more refined then you can apply a drawing fluid first. Place a drawing of the image you want underneath the screen to act as a guide, then trace it very lightly in pencil onto the screen. Using the drawing fluid, paint it on top of where you outlined the image. It is quite important to plot out where you want the image to be before you start painting, as it may end up not fitting onto the screen, or if you should have it too close to the frame of the screen, it will be difficult to print through.

Once the fluid has dried, then you should apply an even coat of screen filler over the top with a squeegee; the drawing fluid will act as a resist. Once this has dried, spray cold water on both sides of the screen to remove the drawing fluid, but leaving the screen filler in place. The screen is then ready for printing.

Other Fillers

Manutex, which is also used to create a print paste with reactive dyes (*refer* to Chapter 7 for an explanation on how to mix it), can be applied to a silk screen to act as resist filler. Paint the Manutex in syrup- like consistency onto the screen; then over-print with your printing ink. Manutex easily washes off the screen with water.

Wax candles or crayons can be drawn onto the mesh to create a resist effect with interesting detailed textures and marks. Use a relatively old screen mesh, as the wax can be difficult to remove with white spirit afterwards.

ABOVE LEFT: **A blank sample silk screen.**

ABOVE: **Paint on Manutex as a resist filler. The Manutex does not need to dry before printing.**

LEFT: **Using a squeegee, pull the printing ink through the screen; the Manutex will resist the ink, leaving a negative print on the printing surface.**

Hand-Painting onto the Silk Screen

If you have a good drawing hand then this method is very useful and can provide the most intricate detailed images, as well as bold painterly marks. Hand-painting the screen mesh can be done on a completely blank silk screen or one where you have exposed basic shapes on it already, which helps to act as a guide to paint within.

There are two methods, one involves printing the ink wet, which creates solid, bold images, and the other is applying dye onto the screen, which can be painted with great detail and printed through when dry. Both methods work equally well on paper and fabric.

The wet method involves using textile inks made up into a medium suitable for printing; either pigment, reactive or acid printing ink will work (*see* Chapter 7). Alternatively, as previously mentioned, you could use an acrylic medium for printing on paper and heavyweight canvases. This process needs to be done all over the screen mesh quickly, unless you have already exposed the basic shapes of images on the screen or used screen filler then this will make the process easier. Firstly, make sure that your silk screen is slightly raised up off the table and paint the ink on the inside of the screen mesh quickly, not allowing the ink to dry on the mesh. Then place the screen onto your fabric or paper, and pull through with a squeegee; this will even out any thicker areas of ink, so the print is flat.

If your screen is blank then you will need to completely block the whole surface area in with ink, otherwise the ink will bleed and colours run into each other when it is being pulled through with a squeegee. This method does require extra speed. If you don't want the print to cover the entirety of your print surface, then you could use a paper stencil placed on top of your paper or fabric to resist areas.

The second method yields the best results using textile dyes mixed with water, and printed through separately using the gums and thickeners that are normally already mixed in when doing conventional printing. Dissolve the dye powder in water, usually hot water to help it dissolve properly. Put much less dye in than you would use for a printing recipe (*see* Chapter 7). Use the dye like watercolours, and paint your images onto the inside of the screen. You do not need to fill the whole space, as the images will not bleed when printed. The ink will look dull at this stage on the mesh, so don't compensate by overpainting; the image will brighten up when printed. Wait for the dye to dry on the mesh of the screen and then print it through with the appropriate thickener that should also contain the correct fixatives if working on fabric. Follow the recipes in Chapter 7 on print pastes and guidance on finishing.

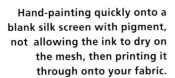

Hand-painting quickly onto a blank silk screen with pigment, not allowing the ink to dry on the mesh, then printing it through onto your fabric.

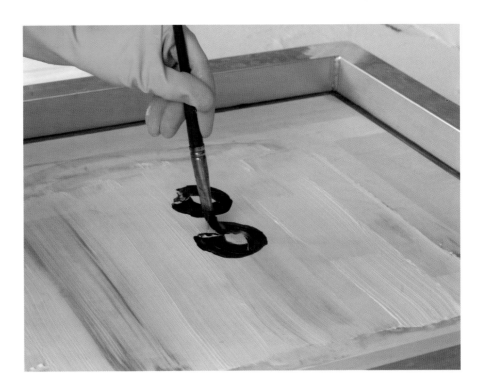

Hand-painting onto a blank silk screen with reactive fabric dyes. Allow the dye to dry before printing.

BELOW: **Hand-painted design on silk fabric, by Asahi Ito. The design was initially painted onto a silk screen with fabric dyes, and printed through when dry.**

The drawback with these methods is that you will only get approximately two or three prints out of each one, the second being much paler. On paper, though, it does enliven your colour palette with the wide variety of dye colours available and is an alternative to using normal paints.

Stencils

If you are unable to have your images exposed onto a silk screen, then making stencils is an alternative way of printing your images. Paper stencils are sufficient if you have a blank silk screen, but may only yield a handful of prints before breaking down. Acetate sheets or another resistant plastic that can be stuck to the screen will last longer, but have no absorbency, so there can sometimes be a thick layer of ink around the edge of your printed image on fabric. You can also buy iron-on stencil paper.

If you are only planning a one-off print, it is probably a good idea to place the cut-out stencil directly on the fabric, so you know exactly where the print is going. If you are planning multiple prints with one image then you should attach the stencil to the back of the screen. Make sure the stencil is not made

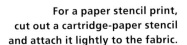

For a paper stencil print, cut out a cartridge-paper stencil and attach it lightly to the fabric.

Place the silk screen on top.

Wood block (*left*) used by Joyce Clissold and printed result (*right*).
(Central St Martins Museum and Study Collection)

onto; an acetate sheet will do, but a small piece of perspex will be more reusable. Water-based block-printing inks give the best results, but it is worth experimenting with textile inks and acrylic paints.

Place about a tablespoon of ink of on the perspex/acetate, and with a roller spread the ink evenly around the sheet. Make sure your ink is not too runny or it will bleed when printed. You may need a few practice prints to work out the best consistency.

Place your printing block on the ink, applying even pressure all over, or the ink take-up will be uneven. Alternatively, use the roller to apply ink directly to your block. Then print on your fabric or paper, applying firm pressure. If working on fabric with textile inks, the fixation and washing-out process will remove uneven ink patches.

If you are planning multiple prints with the same block, first plan out your design in advance lightly drawing out, or masking tape off, exactly where each print is to go.

Monoprinting

Monoprinting transfers bold brush marks, textures and hand-drawn imagery that have been drawn into ink creating both positive and negative prints, onto your paper or fabric surface.

As for block printing you will need thicker inks to avoid bleeding, and some Perspex or acetate and an ink roller.

To create a negative printed image, roll the ink out evenly over the plastic sheet. All the ink will be transferred onto your print surface, so only roll out as much ink as the size you require, or use a variety of colours in different sections. Then use a drawing implement to draw into the ink creating a texture or pattern. The drawing implement can be unconventional such as a twig, bristled brush or wire and so on, as long as it has a reasonably non-porous sharp edge to remove the ink. Then place a sheet of paper on top of the ink image in one movement, and apply gentle pressure all over the back of the paper. You can use a clean roller to gently roll over the back of the paper to help transfer the image evenly, or use the palm of your hand. Remove the paper in one clean movement, so you can do more than one print.

Alternatively, roll out the ink, and simply place a clean piece of paper on top of it, apply no pressure and simply draw on the back of the paper.

If working on fabric, it is easier to work the opposite way and place the inked plastic, directly on to the fabric that is pinned or taped down, particularly if it is a finer fabric. Only apply gentle pressure.

Roll ink onto an acetate sheet for a monoprint.

Draw into the ink.

Place the paper down and gently apply an even pressure.

Carefully peel the paper back.

To create a positive image just draw or paint the ink on to the perspex or acetate in the shape of your desired image. Again you could use multiple colours, and repeat the same process as above.

Resist Printing and Painting

Resists are types of pastes or waxes that act as a barrier against dyes and inks. Patterns and textures can be created by applying forms of resists directly onto your print surface, and then over-printing or painting them. Once the paint or ink is dry the resist is removed, leaving a negative image of your mark-making or drawing behind. Repeated applications of resist and ink or paint should be applied to build up layers of colour.

RESIST ON PAPER

Masking fluid can be used on paper to create similar resist effects to those on fabric. The fluid can be painted on using an ink pen for more linear patterns, or sponged or painted on for bolder designs. Once the fluid has dried then you can apply your dye or printing ink over the top.

When you have finished applying colour, wait for the paper to dry, and gently rub and pull off the masking fluid. Remember to dye the background first, if you do not want any white areas in the design.

Candle wax acts as a resist on paper and can be gently rubbed on; if you place a slightly textured flat surface under the paper, then interesting textures can be picked up.

RESISTS ON FABRIC

Corn and potato dextrin comes in powder form and, when mixed with water, turns into a thick paste that creates a crack-led effect on fabric; it works particularly well on silk. The paste should only be mixed up when you are ready to use it, as it will solidify if left too long, so make sure your fabric is already pinned down to a backing cloth on your print table.

Firstly, dissolve half of the dextrin powder with half of the boiling water. Around 500g of paste is enough to cover about half a metre of fabric, depending on how thick you need to have it.

Spread the paste over the area of fabric. The thicker the paste the larger the cracked effects will be, the thinner the paste the smaller the cracks will appear.

Immediately after applying the dextrin you may wish to draw patterns back into it while it is still pliable – something with an edge such as a fork, or paint-brush handle would be suitable.

Leave the dextrin for half a day to dry out and begin crack-ing. When it has completely cracked, paint or sponge dye over the top, and leave to dry. The dextrin will then fall off, and you will need to steam the fabric for one hour to fix the dye, and then wash the fabric out.

Using dextrin over large areas may be too time-consuming. By using a black dye over the cracked dextrin, the finished result can be photocopied and exposed onto the silk screen.

Paint the dextrin on thickly with a brush.

Draw into it with a sharp edge to create a textured pattern.

Textured pattern using corn dextrin.

Other resist dyeing effects on fabric including wax application can be found in Chapter 6 on dyeing techniques.

Transferring Photocopied Images

There are a range of products on the market, including heat transfer papers and adhesives, that enable the transfer of photocopied images onto your paper and fabric designs. These can be from photographs, computer images, magazines and books. If you are using images from these sources, take care over copyright issues (*see* Chapter 2).

PAPER

If collaging images onto your design is giving unsatisfactory results, most likely because the glued images are not flat enough, then alternatively you can use thinners to transfer black and white images. Black and white pictures can be photocopied, and then transferred with a strong solvent such as cellulose thinners, or acetone. This transfers the black carbon from the copy onto your paper.

Spread the thinners on the back of the photocopy with a cloth, place face down onto the paper, and use a heavy weight to apply pressure; access to a printing press is ideal, as the results will be much sharper. Remember you will need to have your image back to front on the copy for it to transfer the right way round. The drawback to this method is that you will need to use a strong solvent, so make sure your workshop is well-ventilated.

For colour images that may have been printed from the computer or colour photocopies, you will need to transfer the image on to a special paper sometimes called Para-copy or Magic Touch paper. This will need to be done at a specialist photocopiers. Once the image is on the paper, lay it face down onto your design and iron the back of the image at a hot temperature until it has transferred. It will leave a slightly plastic feel to the top of the paper, and may not be suitable on lightweight paper.

FABRIC

Colour photocopied images can be transferred in the same way as on paper above, using transfer papers such as Magic Touch – again it may cockle lightweight fabric.

The solvent method is not really suitable on fabric as the residue is difficult to remove, and keeping lighter-weight fabrics flat enough for transfer is difficult. An alternative method for photocopy transfer is a liquid method sometimes called 'Image Maker'. Place your copy face down onto fabric and spread the image-maker liquid evenly on to the back of the photocopy. After several hours, rub off the paper from the copy on the back, leaving the image transferred on to your fabric. This solution can be bought in most craft stores. Detailed computer

pictures can also be inkjet printed directly on to the fabric (*see* Chapter 4).

HEAT TRANSFER INKS AND PAPERS (SUBLIMATION PRINTING)

Heat transfer inks, or heat transfer papers, are made from a type of dye (Disperse) used to colour synthetic fabrics, and will only work successfully on these (*see* Chapter 6 on dispersal dyeing and transfer). Transfers need to be done at an extremely high temperature, with an iron or heat transfer press. This dry transfer method is an alternative safer method of using these dyes that can also be printed and dyed with.

As well as transferring solid colour and paint marks, the inks or papers also provide a quick and easy method of transferring black and white photocopied images into colour that can then be ironed on to synthetic fabrics. Paler versions are achievable on natural fabrics. Firstly, you need to sponge or paint the heat transfer ink on to blank paper (newsprint will do) and wait for it to dry. You can buy heat transfer papers that are already inked up and ready to use; these are useful if you need an extremely flat colour. This is highly recommended as the painted inks can cockle thin paper, and the colour is transferred slightly unevenly.

Place your inked-up paper face down on to the black and white photocopy, then iron evenly, or place in a heat transfer

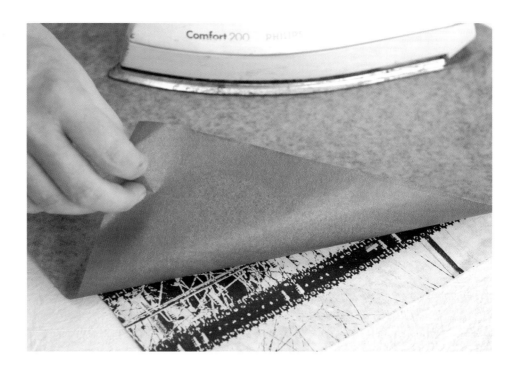

Heat press transfer paper or newsprint painted with heat transfer inks, to a black and white photocopy.

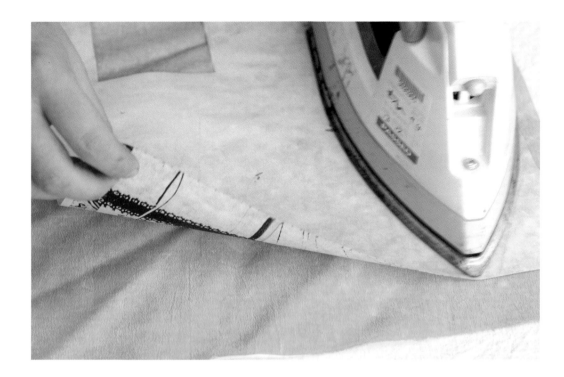

Once ink has been transferred to the photocopy, heat-press it to your synthetic fabric, and this will transfer the image.

press. Transfers for synthetics need to be over 200°C for 30 seconds. This will transfer the ink from the paper on to the carbon of the photocopy. You are then left with a positive and negative image, the positive is the photocopy, and the negative image is the remainder of colour left on the inked-up paper, so you have the option of using both. Then place either of your papers face down on to the fabric and iron or place in the press, and this will transfer the photocopied image (now coloured) or the negative from the inked paper, directly onto your fabric.

Heat transfer inks are versatile and can be used like paints, as well as being bought in crayon and pencil form, so interesting background textures can be made first before transferring onto fabric. Colours can be blended together, or collaged pieces can be assembled directly on the fabric just before transferring.

Flat objects can also be used as a resist between the fabric and the heat transfer paper, to create almost ghostly images on the fabric. Objects such as leaves, thin branches, petals, mesh, threads, feathers and so on or even stencil shapes cut out of paper, are suitable as long as they can resist intense heat. Place your objects on top of the fabric and the coloured heat transfer paper face down and iron. This will transfer the colour leaving an almost x-ray-like negative of your object. If you are using transfer inks then you could paint directly on to your flat objects with textured surfaces, and when dry, place the object ink side down onto your fabric and heat press, to get a positive transfer of your image instead.

Heat Transfer Resist

Heat transfer can be combined with resist print methods to produce easily obtainable and highly effective results. Once you have inked up your paper with heat transfer ink and allowed it to dry (or used heat transfer papers), use a silk screen with photo stencil images to print Indulca thickener directly onto your paper. When the Indulca has dried, it will act as a resist. The paper can then be heat transferred onto your fabric, leaving white images where the Indulca has resisted, and colouring the rest of the fabric.

All these methods are quick and easy to use and it is worth looking for a variety of interesting synthetic fabrics if you wish to use these techniques extensively.

Polyester can give off fumes when heated to high temperatures, so make sure it's done in a well-ventilated area. To protect your iron and table or heat press, use thin paper underneath the fabric and on top of the heat transfer inked paper to keep the surfaces clean.

Place flat objects on your synthetic fabric, to act as a resist to heat transfer.

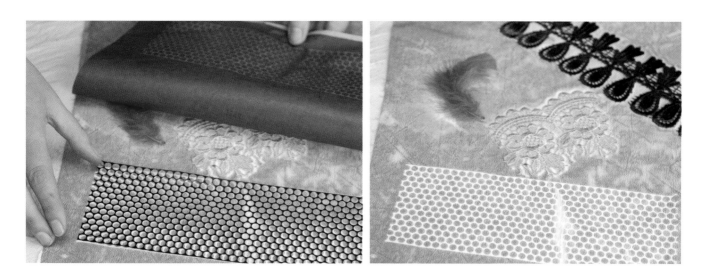

Iron the transfer paper over the top of the objects, revealing
the negative of the image on the fabric underneath.

OPPOSITE PAGE:
**Resisted stitches on polyester using
heat transfer, by Sharifa Syed-Nahar.**

THIS PAGE:
**Resisted feathers on polyester using
heat transfer, by Margaret Campbell.**

Collage, Intercutting and Appliqué

COLLAGE

If you have tried most of the techniques in this chapter already, then you will have a huge selection of designs and patterning techniques to choose from for a final collection. You may decide that some look weak on their own but would work well combined with elements of other designs, and you may wish to experiment with your composition.

If you are working on thin or untextured paper such as cartridge then you can cut out pieces from one design and collage them directly on top of areas of another design, or make a completely collaged piece. If you are using glue, then use a paper glue stick and not a liquid glue that can easily become messy and sometimes not stick the paper down evenly. As soon as you have glued your collage, put a weight on top of it, such as a heavy book, to make sure the images are stuck down fully. Spray mount is good, but only in a well-ventilated area.

INTERCUTTING

Collaging, particularly if the paper is thick and has been glued onto another design, can sometimes look unprofessional and may not hold together. An alternative method of combining different paper images is to intercut the images of one design to replace areas of another design. You will need a very sharp scalpel, masking tape and a cutting mat or drawing board that does not have too many cuts or grooves in it that could affect the cutting of accurate lines.

Before you start, be definite about where you want the images to go, as you will be cutting out areas of the original design, and completely replacing sections of it. Be careful not to have awkward breaks in the replacement design section, as it is crucial for the replacement piece to fit exactly into the gap that has been created. It is definitely worth having a few practice runs at this, as cutting accurately can be difficult until you have improved your technique and, if you have made a mistake, it can be incredibly difficult to salvage the design.

Firstly you need to cut out the replacement image to the right size. Place the single cut-out image on top of the area of the design you want to replace, with masking tape, so it is held down lightly. Place on top of a cutting mat and then, very carefully using the replacement image as a guide, cut with a scalpel around the section of design underneath to the exact size of the replacement image.

When intercutting, put the replacement image in the right position on your design, cut around it carefully, and gently attach it to the design.

BELOW LEFT: **Turn the design over, and remove the cut-out section of the original design.**

BELOW: **Sellotape the new design section to the main design, and check there are no gaps around the edges.**

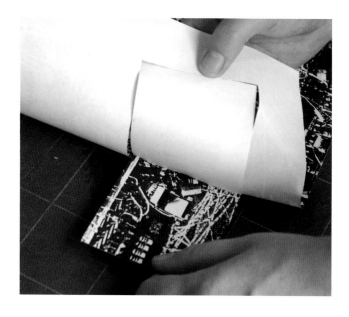

Before removing the old image from underneath, secure the new one to the design by lightly attaching it with small pieces of masking tape. Be gentle about this, otherwise you risk tearing the design when you want to remove the tape.

With the old image removed, carefully turn the design over, and use clear tape to secure the new design along all its edges. Use the bottom end of your scalpel, and run it along the joins to smooth the paper as much as possible, and fill in any tiny gaps.

APPLIQUÉ

To create the same collage effects on fabric using appliqué or patchwork techniques is a good option. Students and designers working in printed textiles very often use these methods, which add another dimension to their prints and an extra sell-

ing point to their work. This can create an extra workload, so do not overburden yourself if you have a tight deadline.

Appliqué is a way of attaching small pieces of fabric on to a background fabric, using stitch or adhesive. You may want to print or dye the background fabric, initially. If you are intending to appliqué on several weighty pieces of fabric make sure the background cloth isn't too sheer or lightweight, or it will hang badly and buckle under the weight of the added materials. Think of the end function for the fabric as well – heavily appliquéd fabrics may be uncomfortable to wear and impractical in the home, if needing continual washing.

Printing images onto your appliqué fabrics first, before cutting them out and attaching them, will give you more variety with patterning options. Printing, particularly outlines of your shape with pigment ink, will aid your fabric cutting, as it creates

Hand-printed and appliquéd skirt, by Nadia Parsons.

a harder, solid edge to the fabric, which makes it easier to cut around and stops the edges from fraying. Alternatively, you may have to hem or overlock the edges of the appliqué pieces to stop them fraying with wear and tear.

The appliqué pieces can be attached to the backing fabric, by stitching all the way around the edge, or just applying a few stitches in the middle, to give a slightly raised effect or overlapping feature with other fabrics. 3D images can be created with stiffer fabrics, or fabric with wire hemmed into it. Patchwork will cover the entire piece, and you have the option of sandwiching wadding in the middle to create a stitched quilted effect.

If stitching is not one of your strongest skills, then apply a heat transferable glue such as Bondaweb that is sticky on both sides. Bondaweb is the brand name for a very useful and versatile adhesive that is mainly used for attaching fabrics together for layering, mending and reinforcing purposes. Bondaweb is bought in flat sheets in different strengths, so can easily be cut to the right size, and is ironed on to stick permanently to fabric.

Make sure the surface of the fabric is clean of any debris, then cut the Bondaweb roughly to the shape of the piece you are going to stick on. Iron the glue side down to the fabric shape. Cut the appliqué and attached Bondaweb to the exact size, and peel off the Bondaweb's protective sheet on the back. Place the exposed glue side down onto the backing fabric and iron on. A Teflon sheet in between the heat source and Bondaweb is useful to protect from melted glue attaching itself to the iron. Teflon can be wiped clean easily. Alternatively some lining fabrics have a dry layer of glue on one side that immediately sticks with heat.

Stitch

Stitching directly onto your design can also create interesting textured patterns on both paper and fabric. A portable sewing machine is a good investment if you are interested in developing stitch and embellishment effects, and useful for making finished sellable goods. Using an embroidery needle on the machine will allow you to draw detailed patterns and images in multiple colours in stitch on both paper and fabric. Colour papers and fabrics can be stitched on randomly at the same time, for more solid areas.

Stitching the patterns with black thread onto white paper or fabric, gives you the option of transferring the images onto silk screen and printing. The stitched design will need to be photocopied clearly in black. This will capture the mark-making created by the stitching, and can be an alternative quicker method on large fabric pieces that are too time consuming to cover in embroidery.

Hand-stitching on fabric is a very good way of imitating drawing marks and lines from paperwork designs, and you can experiment with the widths and lengths of the thread.

Even if you have printed your fabrics, stitching or embellishment on top can add highlights that provide finishing touches to lift the overall appearance of the design. All fabrics and paper can be stitched on. It is recommended that you use an embroidery ring to give you more control when stitching on lighter fabrics. Experimenting with colourful threads, beading, sequins and so on, will create interesting textures, and give a more sumptuous look to your fabrics.

If you are interested in manipulating the fabric shape and creating more 3D effects, then heavy layers of embroidery, smocking and pleating techniques can add extra depth to your work. Using elastic thread in your machine will also create a puckered fabric effect.

Delicate embroidered patterns can be achieved by using dissolvable fabrics as a backing to stitch on to. These are plastic in feel, and work better in an embroidery ring. Once you have stitched your patterns, the fabric can be dissolved in either hot or cold water, leaving just the embroidered thread behind. The thread pattern can be exposed directly onto a silk screen for printing, or used with heat transfer inks on synthetic fabrics, to make a positive transfer or negative resist.

Flock, Foils and Glitter

Flock, foil paper and glitter can all be used as embellishments on fabric and paper, with the aid of a water-based adhesive. Flock paper is traditionally associated with decorative wallpapers, creating a relief fabric effect, but works just as well on fabric as wallpaper. The flock can be bought by the roll attached to a paper backing, which is preferable to loose flock fibres floating around the environment. White is sufficient as it can be coloured with hand-painted dyes for cellulose fibres.

For all the products you should firstly print or paint the water-based glue onto your surface and wait for it to dry.

Place a sheet of flock paper, on top of and covering all the glue areas you have printed, making sure it is flock side down onto your glue surface. Iron or heat press the back of the flock paper for one minute at 180°C. When the flock and glue has cooled down, peel off the backing paper and excess flock, to reveal the flock print underneath.

Foil paper creates a metallic colour effect, and can be bought in sheets from craft suppliers. There are interesting iridescent colours in the foil range, as well as flat colours. Print and wait for the glue to dry again before applying your foil colour-side up, on

Once you have heat-pressed the flock paper to the dried glue print, wait for it to cool down before peeling back the flock paper.

BELOW: **Creating a slightly raised surface using flock paper.**

your paper or fabric. Place a Teflon sheet or sheet of paper over the top of the foil before ironing or heat pressing, or it will melt. The temperature should be 180°C for 30 seconds. Allow the foil to cool down before peeling off the excess.

For glitter effects on fabric, apply the glue in the same way as above, and sprinkle your glitter on, before heat-setting it.

The disadvantage of the methods above is for multi-washing purposes: water-based glue will not be long lasting, so you may have to switch to an alternative solvent-based glue.

Textured and Uneven Patterns on Paper and Fabric

You may be interested in using textures and slightly raised surfaces as part of the theme of your design work. On paper, thicker textured marks and patterns can be achieved by using oil paints, block-printing inks and acrylics that are much thicker

Place a piece of foil over the dry glue, and heat-press the foil, using a protective surface in between.

Once it has cooled down, peel the excess foil away.

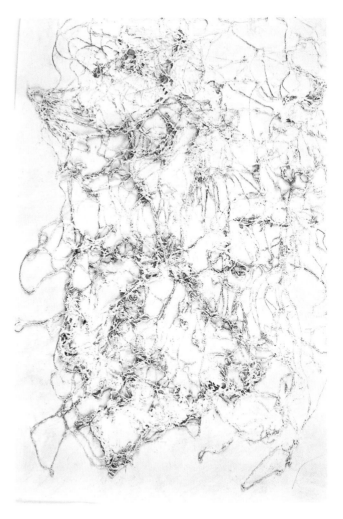

in consistency. These can be applied with bold brush strokes and block-printing methods. PVA glue can be painted on or used to glue down tissue paper, sweet wrappers, sand, sawdust and so on onto paper to create uneven surfaces.

Acrylic paints also have a wide variety of different textured mediums. These include a gloss effect, a gritty black lava, blended fibres, ceramic stucco, and a shiny glass bead. These can be mixed in with acrylic colours and painted onto paper and fabric only if a stiff surface is not a problem, and they do not need washing as part of their end function.

Textured paper design using string, by Sharifa Syed-Nahar.

**Paper burnt out with joss sticks to create
a patterned texture effect, by Asahi Ito.**

can be used to puncture and draw patterns very effectively on paper, particularly on an already patterned paper. A hole puncher is also effective, and different colour papers can be attached behind the punctured piece, to allow layers of colours to show through.

Layers of fabric can be stitched, glued or laminated together, and then be cut, distressed, frayed or burnt back to reveal the various layers below, creating exciting textures. Laser cutting is a completely controlled way of creating burnt-out pattern structures designed on computer (*see* Chapter 4).

Devoré is another controlled method of burning away different types of fabric that can be hand applied (*see* Chapter 7). It is mainly used on mixed-fibre fabrics to burn away one type of fibre, but can burn holes straight through or skim the surface of heavyweight fabrics made from one type of fibre. Velvet, corduroy and felt produce successful results.

Bleaching and Discharging Inks and Dyes

Bleaching and discharging are useful techniques if you want to work back into dark colour grounds, avoiding the use of layers of thick opaque ink on top, particularly if you are working on more delicate papers and fabrics. Some designers also find working from a blank white sheet of paper or fabric quite daunting, and have an existing background colour already there, to make it easier to work from.

You may wish to dye your own background colours, which is better, as you can do tests to see which colours bleach and discharge well. Indian inks and fabric dyes are the best to use on paper, and fabric dyes that are compatible for different types of fabric.

If this is not appropriate for your fabric, then there is a range of special textile binders that create similar effects. They are water-based pigment binders and include gloss, glitter, pearl, thick opaque and 3D effects that can all be screen-printed (*see* Chapter 4). All these textile inks can be used on paper as well, except for puff binder (3D) as it will break off a paper surface.

As well as adding texture on top of your paper and fabric, the surface of your design can be worked back into to create uneven surface effects.

Puncturing holes and making uneven layers through burning and tearing your paper can also create textured surfaces and patterns. A sewing machine needle with no thread in it

BLEACHING

Household bleach is fine to use, thicker bleaches may give you more control if you are painting it on directly, or you may want to water it down to create a less noticeable colour change and a more washed out look. All the dye colours will react almost immediately and differently, so you may find some unexpected exciting results.

Once you have bleached out sections, you may have to switch to a pigment or acrylic-based ink if you want to work back on top, as any new dye will probably continually disappear on the bleached areas. Acrylic can also be mixed with bleach, removing the background colour, and instantaneously

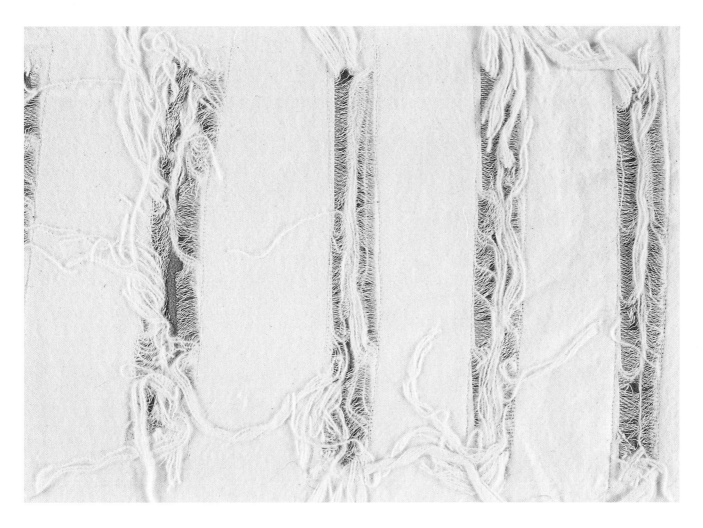

Distressed textured fabric effect, by Natalie Hand.

replacing it with another acrylic colour. This follows the same principle as discharging fabric.

On fabric after bleaching, you will need to wash out the material carefully in diluted acetic acid or white vinegar, to neutralize the effects of the bleach to stop the fabric eventually rotting.

DISCHARGING

Discharge is a screen printable paste that can take the fabric back to its original white state, or remove the coloured background and replace it with another colour. Very detailed images can be obtained by screen-printed methods, making it favourable over bleach.

Only certain dyed colours are susceptible to being stripped out by discharge chemicals, so you will definitely need to test the colours out first (*see* Chapters 6 and 7). Once you have printed, painted or sponged on the paste, you will be unable to see your results until the samples have been dried and steamed, which can make it difficult to work out your colours and composition on the print table. The results, particularly on silk, yield very intense, bright colours.

Paper discharge prints can be ironed out, but this can be unsuitable if there is little ventilation in your work space, as the fumes given off are very strong. Only a controlled steaming environment for fabric discharge, provides protection from the fumes.

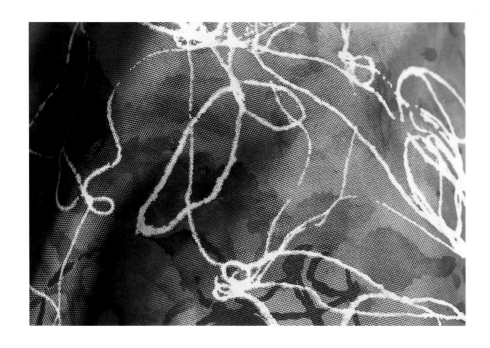

Discharge printed lining in jacket, by Sharifa Syed-Nahar.

BELOW: **Mood board for design project by Nadia Parsons.**

Care does need to be taken over both these products. Make sure your room is well-ventilated, and only work for short periods of time.

Presenting and Mounting Paper and Fabric Designs

How you present your work, whether it is for a gallery exhibition, commercial design brief or student project, can make a huge difference to how it is viewed. Cleanly and simply presented work reflects care and pride in what you are doing and a high standard of professionalism. Sloppy presentation allows the eye to be distracted from the design piece itself. The first thing anyone will notice before even seeing your design is warped unstretched papers, frayed fabric edges, and both fabrics and paper that are not cut at straight angles.

There is no need to go for elaborate presentations that will also distract from your main design. Always mount your work on paper or card in neutral colours – white or grey are best to use.

Mood Boards

These are important for collating your source material, and possibly a way of selling the theme or ideas to a company. A mood board is a collage of fabric swatches, sketches, photographic images, colour palettes and even text.

Make sure you use good quality card (A2 is a good size to use), and that the work is securely attached to the mount with either paper glue or spray mount. The information and samples should be carefully distributed around the board, with as much care over composition as your design work. Try and place everything creatively and in an informative way, and if you do not have tidy handwriting, use letraset, or typed material.

Paper Designs

If you have produced a collection of designs to give to an agent, or directly to a company, then they will probably expect you to mount everything on medium-weight white cartridge paper. Choose one size of mounting paper, again A2 is good; don't use card or thicker paper, otherwise the combined weight of this with all your other mounted designs will be too heavy to carry around. Make sure you firstly trim your design, to lose any

scuffed edges, and make sure the design is cut at complete right angles. A triangle and a metal ruler will help you with this.

The design only needs to be attached to its mount at the top, as it will probably need to be remounted occasionally, and companies will like to place the design directly against a product such as clothing to get a better idea of its potential use.

When mounting, place a strip of masking tape or Sellotape along the top edge of the back of the design. This will always protect your design from tearing if you need to change the mount.

Attach two small pieces of double-sided tape about 3cm long, on top of the Sellotape or masking tape at either end. Then attach the top of the design to your white paper mount. Place it as centrally as possible; this can be done by eye.

Mounting Fabric

Your finished fabric samples should be ironed carefully, and then cut at straight right angles. You can use tailor's chalk lightly to draw in the straight lines. On medium- to heavyweight fabrics put a strip of a clear tape such as Scotch tape around all the edges of the back of the fabric, as this will make it easier to cut straight lines through, and prevent the fabric from fraying.

This can be difficult with sheer or silky fabrics that slip and move easily, so hemming will be easier. If you have access to an overlocker machine, this will sew over the edges to prevent fraying, and also trim off non-straight edges at the same time. Otherwise, hem the edges by ironing a straight, single or double fold around the sides of the fabrics and machine-stitch the fold in straight lines using thread the same colour as the background fabric. Try not to let the stitching encroach too much into the design. The fabric then just needs to be mounted with a header of a folded overpiece of card along the top, so clients can hold the fabric by the mount, preventing the fabric from being creased when being viewed.

Already manufactured headers can be bought, from fashion retail suppliers, but it is also easy to make your own. You will need to cut a piece of white card to the exact width of your fabric sample, and about 12cm in depth. Carefully score the card with a scalpel all the way across the middle of the width of the card, at about 6cm, so it folds in half exactly. Make sure you don't cut too deeply before folding the card in half at the scored line. Stick double-sided tape to the inside edges of the folded card, all along the width. Slip the fabric inside and attach it to the card as straight as possible, and then close it.

It is worth buying mounts with hangers attached if your samples are for an exhibition, so they can easily be hung on a rail.

CHAPTER 4

COMBINING OLD AND NEW

The rapid improvements in industrial technology regarding the manufacture of new fabrics and methods of surface pattern application have now filtered down to student level, and you will need to be aware of new performance fabrics, printing and patterning equipment, and print and dye materials. Designing on computer and digitally printing fabrics is now commonplace in education as well as the workplace.

This does not mean the beginning of the end of hand-crafted processes though, as these methods of working are becoming integrated with modern materials, and used in combination with newer techniques. There will always be a market for the handmade product, and whilst technology cannot create a substitute, it should be embraced as an opportunity for developing innovations. This chapter will show how some collaborations have occurred between traditional methods and new technology.

At a local level it is obviously impossible financially and technically to equip yourself to the same standards as industry, but some companies and colleges hire out specific specialized equipment for students and designers to use. There is always the possibility of collaboration as well. Companies will often sponsor a student or designer's work, by providing materials in return

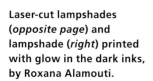

Laser-cut lampshades (*opposite page*) and lampshade (*right*) printed with glow in the dark inks, by Roxana Alamouti.

for any creative or experimental results using their product. Many large industrial companies and manufacturers have little artistic and creative input, and may welcome the creative inventions and alternative uses of their products.

Designing on Computer and Digital Printing

If you are intending to work in industry, then it is important to have a good knowledge of Computer Aided Design, as many companies now design solely on computer. Many colleges offer short courses in Photoshop, Illustrator or specific courses

OPPOSITE PAGE:
Digitally printed coat, by Aya Tsukai.

Cotton fabric being digitally printed with reactive inks, by Nicky Gearing at London College of Fashion. (Photograph by June Fish)

in designing for textiles that will get you up to speed. Digital printing is still only a small part of the printed textile market but this will change in the future, as it will become more cost-effective than other printing methods. There are limitations at the moment as the printers are slow, and only conventional printing inks can be used. Finishing methods (*see* Chapter 7) still need to be carried out manually, but these processes are continually improving.

If you are working at home and are unable to set up a conventional hand-printing workshop space, or cannot access facilities locally, then designing on computer is an ideal solution. If you need to print out your design work onto either fabric or paper then your disc containing the designs can be sent off to a digital printers where they will do the printout work for you. If you have a sensitivity to using textile dyes and inks directly, and are worried about them affecting your health, designing on computer is an alternative safe way of working.

Make sure your computer program provides a variety of drawing and painting implements, and a wide-ranging colour palette. A scanner is also essential for helping to manipulate hand-drawn designs that can be scanned in and reworked. Photos, book and magazine images can also be scanned and integrated to fit in with your own drawings and colour schemes. Easy variations and manipulations of your design can be carried out by trying it in different formats such as 3D relief or mosaic style, or completely altering the colour palette. Colours are now becoming more compatible with printing inks and dyes. All the different versions of your design can be easily stored on disc and kept for use later on.

Working on the computer has a huge advantage over paper-work designing as it allows you to quickly try out different design compositions and structures before settling on one you prefer, including putting images into repeat. There are a variety of programs to help with different repeat structures for patterns, such as half drop and brick repeat. A digital printer can also print out your design in repeat over several metres of fabric.

If you are using CAD to help you design for eventual hand-printing with a silk screen, then Photoshop can also separate the colours out, and then print them individually as black positives, necessary for exposure onto silk screen.

Some fabric companies now sell a range of materials already prepared for digitally printing onto. Alternatively, the actual digital printers will supply their own range of fabrics; you will need to check this out with your printing company. The fabric is prepared for digital printing by already being impregnated with chemicals and fixatives, so it is just necessary for the dye to be inkjet printed on. Digital printing inks are the standard ones

Laser Cutting

Laser cutting is a relatively new technology which involves cutting or etching patterned shapes out of fabric and some other hard materials such as glass, metal and plastics. The layout for the surface-pattern design can be drawn using Illustrator or Coreldraw computer programs, and then etched or cut by a carbon laser.

The best fabrics to use for cutting are polyester, silk, wool, leather and acetate, as the laser is able to fuse the edges of the fabric, preventing fraying. Completely cut-through fabrics are useful for products such as lampshades, or for layered fabrics and 3D effects.

For etching denim, fleece, suede and leather, all work well, and create a similar effect to devoré printing. Laser cutting is viewed as an alternative method of patterning to more environmentally hazardous methods with dyes and inks, although it is at the moment an expensive process to carry out.

Laminating

Laminating is used to describe a process of applying layers to fabrics, by attaching two or more pieces of fabric together. This can be achieved through stitching, or using a fabric adhesive such as Bondaweb (Chapter 3). If you are using sheer transparent fabrics for laminating together, then it is possible to trap small 2D objects such as petals or threads and so on to create patterns in the middle that can be seen through both sides.

Colour plastic can also be melted and stuck together in collaged layers, to create interesting plastic patterning effects. A clear pliable plastic, called hot melt film, is available and sticks directly to paper or fabric without any need for an adhesive, creating a shiny plastic coating on the surface. Again, 2D flat objects can be trapped inside to create visible patterns.

For laminating with plastic, your heat source – either an iron or heat press – should be at a temperature of 120°C; if it is too hot, the plastic or film will disintegrate. Also place a sheet of Teflon (which can be bought at a supermarket) over the top of the plastic, to stop the plastic having direct contact, and melting onto the heat source.

Another book in the Crowood series on textiles by Jac Scott called *Textile Perspectives in Mixed-Media Sculpture* gives good practical tips and examples on laminating and using equipment such as a heat gun and soldering iron, if this is an area you wish to explore.

Pattern created by laminating plastics together, by Nadia Parsons.

used for screen-printing, including reactives, acids and heat transfer inks. What ink is used depends on the type of fabric you are working with (*refer* to Chapters 5 or 7). The digital printing company usually takes care of the finishing processes such as baking, steaming and washing, otherwise you will have to do this yourself if you are only having the actual printing done. The finishing processes are the same as those for hand-printing.

If you do have the opportunity of using both hand-applied printing and patterning, and digital methods, then this is an excellent opportunity to utilize the best qualities of both. Digital printing produces incredibly detailed images that are not easily accessible even to screen printing, but can only print in a very flat method with little tactility. Embellishing or hand-applying motifs and images on top of the digital image by printing or stitching can provide extra texture and depth to the fabric, giving it a unique look.

Thermoplastics

This is used to describe materials that, when heated, become soft and pliable and can be moulded into shape before being cooled and becoming hard again. These qualities are found in plastics and synthetic fabrics that have similar molecular structures.

Some synthetic fabrics have also been impregnated with resins at the manufacturing stage and can be shaped. The fabric will generally need to be at least two thirds synthetic for any moulding and shaping techniques to work. Polyester is generally a good fabric to use.

Contemporary Japanese fashion and textile designers have been some of the most innovative in recent times, in this field. They have quite often married ancient crafts and techniques with modern materials and processes to create brand new fabric patterns and constructions. The work of designers such as Jun'ichi Arai and Nuno fabrics, and Issey Miyake is worth exploring more in depth for research into moulded fabrics.

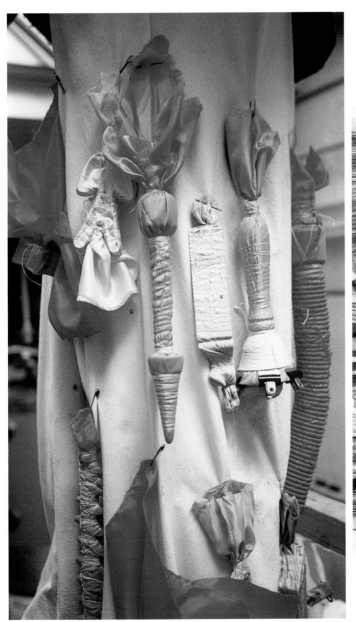

LEFT: **Polyester woven fabrics wrapped around solid objects ready to go into the steamer, to create 3D permanent effects, by Frederique Denniel.**

ABOVE: **The resulting 3D effect, by Frederique Denniel.**

Polyester fabric, bonded together using ultrasonic welding technology, by Davina Hawthorne. (Photograph by Othello de Souza Hartley)

BELOW LEFT: **Crinkled and heat-transferred coloured polyester**, by Sarah Wilson.

Shibori Dye Techniques with Synthetic Fibres

An interesting example of how old and new techniques have combined, has been the use of ancient Japanese Shibori dyeing techniques, used to mould and heat-set synthetic materials. Polyester and acetate give the best results. The fabric should be tied, wrapped or clamped in the usual way (*see* Chapter 6 for a range of Shibori techniques), and then either steamed for approximately 20–30min, or boiled in water in a stainless steel dye vat for about 20min. If you are using the latter method, then this also gives you the option of dyeing the fabric at the same time with dispersal dyes. If using the technique of wrapping the fabric around a pole, make sure you use wood or heat-proof plastic, and tie any metal clamps with a long piece of string hanging over the side of the vat of boiling water, to allow you to remove the clamp without handling it.

To create pleats or reasonably flat folds in the fabric, then heat-setting it with an iron or in a heat press is sufficient. The fabric folds can be held in place by being wrapped in tin foil, which should be contained between each fold or pleat. The iron or press should be at a temperature of 200°C, and pressed for 1min. Remember to use a Teflon sheet to prevent direct contact with the heat source, or the fabric will melt. If using a dry heat to mould your fabric, you have the option of transferring colour on at the same time by using heat transfer papers (*see* Chapter 3).

Once the fabric has been set, it will remain permanent unless it is reshaped at the same temperature.

Embossing

Paper can be embossed by applying pressure with a printing press over slightly raised objects underneath damp paper. Similar results can be achieved on particular synthetic fabrics, such as acetate satin and synthetic felt. These can be moulded to create slightly embossed raised effects using the heat of an iron, or a heat press. To protect your table surface from being damaged by the heat, Bulgomme fabric is traditionally used to act as a heat

barrier. Embossing mats are also useful if you have a heat press, for applying extra pressure to mould the fabric. Place an embossing mat on the bottom, with relatively flat objects placed on top such as string, coins, cardboard, mesh and so on, followed by the synthetic fabric. Apply the heat source for 1min at 200°C. The impression of the object left on the fabric will remain permanent, unless it is reset at the same temperature.

Printing Inks with Special Effects

Speciality inks that create different effects are now easily available and can be applied using traditional screen-printed methods or by hand-painting. Many art and craft shops stock small quantities of many of these inks if you want to experiment first. Most of

Embossed pins on synthetic felt, by Sarah Wilson.

the inks are water based, and can be fixed and finished in the same way as regular water-based pigment (*see* Chapter 7). These include the following:

Heat-Sensitive Ink

This ink is similar in quality to pigment and uses the same binder, and is screen-printed or hand-painted onto fabric. The ink changes colour with a fluctuation of temperature, particularly after being touched.

UV-Sensitive Ink

This is also a water-based pigment sharing the same binder as regular pigment, and is charged by ultraviolet light, which creates a 'glow in the dark' effect.

Aromatic Ink

These inks can be added into a pigment binder and, when scratched, release a variety of aromatic smells.

Opaque Binder

If you wish to print lighter colours onto darker colour dyed backgrounds, then you will need to switch from standard pigment binder to an opaque binder that will sit on top of dark colours. The binder is very thick, so you can combine it with standard binder to reduce the stiffness of the fabric.

Gloss Binder

On its own, gloss binder creates a shiny almost plastic print on your fabric, similar to acrylic gloss. It can be mixed directly with pigment colour, but can clog up silk screens because of its thick consistency.

Pearl Binder

Pearl binder is mixed with standard pigment colours, turning them metallic. It is also opaque.

Glitter Binder

A water-based pigment ink that produces a shimmering glitter print effect.

Puff Binder

A water-based pigment that can be mixed with standard colour, and expands under heat to create 3D effects with a rubbery texture. Puff binder can be printed in the normal way, and when it is dry the fabric is placed in a baking cabinet, or a heat press. Do not lower the hot plate from the press onto the fabric, as direct contact with the print will immediately flatten the puff binder. You can also use an iron carefully on the back of the fabric. On stretchy fabric like cotton jersey, the raised print can also create an embossed effect on the other side, or on non-stretch fabrics can pucker and gather the fabric up.

White Binder

This binder can be used on its own to make a strong luminous white effect on dark colours. Again this ink has a thick consistency and can be diluted with standard binder to reduce the stiffness and cracking of the ink on fabric.

Goldbinder and Metallic Colours

To produce pigment colours in gold, silver, bronze and so on, you will need a specialist metallic binder and metallic powder colour. Powdered colours are slightly more hazardous than in a liquid state, so should be mixed in a fume cupboard, or in a well-ventilated area, while wearing a dust mask. The ratio of binder to powder is: 100g of gold binder to 20g metallic powder. Printing and fixing are then exactly the same as other pigment methods.

Elasticil

If you are printing onto stretchy fabrics, most pigment inks are not pliable and will crack when stretched, so elasticil binder has been created to stretch with your fabric.

Puff binder, creating a 3D effect on cotton jersey fabric, by Margaret Campbell.

Conductive Textiles

If you are interested in the future development and function of textiles, then conductive fabrics is an area to look into. Already the textile industry is developing and experimenting with fabric that contains electrical equipment embedded in the fabric, but is still lightweight enough to wear. Electrical charges can be sent around the material that can operate built-in equipment such as mobile phones, stereos and so on. Fibre optics and glass fibres have also been developed that can transmit light, and send digital information around a circuit. Successful results have been achieved by printing superconducting circuits onto fabric, using conventional screen-printing methods. Once printed, the circuits are able to burn away the organic binder they were printed with, and provide antennae for radio reception, and filters for cell phones in the fabric. This work was carried out by the University of Linz, in Austria, and offers a potential future use for traditional printing methods.

Metal in fibres can also send electrical charges through clothing, which can be used to control the temperature of the fabric, and warn against environmental hazards. Many of these innovations have been developed at NASA, for use in space suits, and research into medical fabrics and high-performance jobs and sports such as motor racing.

The future of fabrics will most definitely include the use of digital technology in clothing and accessories, and fabrics with multi-functional uses.

CHAPTER 5

IDENTIFYING FABRICS AND FIBRES FOR PRINTING AND DYEING

FIBRE TYPES

Cellulose fibres are all made from plant material and include:

▪ Cotton, Linen, Jute, Hemp, Sisal

Reconstituted cellulose fibres are produced by man-made methods, using reconstituted cellulose. They have similar properties to cotton, and can be dyed and printed in the same way. These include:

▪ Viscose Rayon, Acetate Rayon, Tencel and Modal

Protein fibres are animal-based and mostly made from animal hair. These include:

▪ Wool, Cashmere, Mohair, Angora and Silk

Synthetic fibres are mainly made from oil and coal and include:

▪ Polyester, Polyamide (Nylon) and Acrylic

There are many variations and brand names for these materials.

The fabric you use to print or pattern on, will have a big impact on the look, function and durability of your textile designs, so it is hugely important to use the most relevant material. This chapter will give you background knowledge of fabric and fibre types, including their practical qualities, to enable you to choose the most applicable type of fabric for the patterning effects and the functional uses you wish to achieve. Chapter 3 looked briefly at the visual characteristics, styles and weights of fabric available, so remember to cross-reference while looking through this chapter.

It is important to take your fabric knowledge one stage further than purely its visual qualities for two main reasons: firstly, most dyes and printing inks will only work with certain fibre types so you will need to identify the original source of the fabric. Secondly, if you are making finished textile products you will require specific qualities from the fabric such as, durability, elasticity, coolness or absorbency, and so on.

The first criteria to establish is whether the fabric is from a natural source; either plant based (cellulosic fibre), animal based (protein fibre) or a man-made, synthetic source.

The box (*left*) breaks down fibre types into their main categories, and lists a selection of fabrics from each group.

Identifying Fibres

The list above clearly defines each fibre type from the source it has come from, but different fibres can be woven or knitted in the same way to look identical to each other as fabrics. Many of the fabrics listed in Chapter 3 are good examples of this. For example, organza can be made from polyester, cotton or silk, so

Pleated and printed silk fabric, by Nicola Sergiou.

you will need to be clear about what you are buying. Buy your fabric from a reputable supplier who gives a clear indication of what the fabric is made from, to save wasting your time and money. Make sure you are able to obtain enough fabric for the job at hand, and that it will not go out of stock if you need more in the future.

Once you have experience of handling a wide variety of fabrics, you will gradually develop your skill at identifying the fabric type, so you can experiment with more unusual fabrics from different sources, such as recycled materials. There are several tests you can do yourself to help identify the fibre type.

Handle of the Fabric

Rubbing the fabric in your hand often gives a good indication if a fabric is natural or synthetic, as many synthetics are stiffer and crispier in feel. The edge or tear of a fabric can also give a good clue, as synthetics often have a rougher shredded edge.

Water Repellence

Synthetics are more water repellent than natural fibres, and if you splash some water on the fabric and it runs off easily without absorbing, you will be able tell if it is either man-made or coated with a finish such as wax. Some natural fibres also come in a more raw state such as wool, and natural oils will also act as a barrier to water.

Sight and Smell of the Fabric

Cellulose fibres such as cotton often have a duller look than regenerated cellulose fibres, which are shinier in appearance, such as viscose. Wool can often be yellowish in colour or will smell of fleece particularly when wet. Raw silks have a strong odour, and are more textured, compared to processed silks. Silk has a more sophisticated look than its synthetic imitations. Mixed-fibre fabrics are hard to distinguish, but can sometimes be identified by their contrasting fibres such as polyester and metallic yarn mix, or cotton and goat's hair mix.

Burns Testing

If you are still unable to identify your fabric, then burning a small piece gives away many fibre characteristics, although again mixed fibre fabrics will be hard to distinguish. The table (*below*) gives an indication of what to look out for.

BURN TESTING

FABRIC	SPEED OF BURNING	TYPE OF BURN	COLOUR	ODOUR
COTTON	fast	Grey ash, continues burning after flame is removed	Yellow flame	Burning paper
LINEN	fast	Grey ash, burns less after flame is removed	Yellow flame	Burning paper
SILK	slow	Irregular, then may self-extinguish	Bluish flame	Burning hair or feathers
WOOL	slow	Irregular then may self-extinguish	Bluish flame	Burning hair or feathers
VISCOSE RAYON	fast	Regular, leaves greyish ash	Grey flame	Burning paper
ACETATE RAYON	slow	Creates crushable beads that shrink from the flame	Grey flame	Vinegar, burnt paper
POLYESTER	Hard to ignite, then medium to fast	Melts, leaving hard black beads	Yellow flame	Aromatic, sweet smell
ACRYLIC	Very fast	Melts, leaving hard black beads	Bright flame	Acrid smell
NYLON	Medium to fast	Melts, leaving hard light-brown beads	Grey flame	Celery

Fabric Qualities

Below are a selection of the fabric types you are more likely to use, with their characteristics and functional abilities, and print and dye possibilities. Remember other fabrics listed in the same fibre categories will also work with the same print and dye methods.

COTTON

Examples of dyed and printed cotton can be found from thousands of years ago, in many parts of the world, and it is still the most widely-used fibre today. Cotton is extremely practical because it is strong, cool and moisture absorbent, which makes it ideal for garments. It is heat-resistant and can be laundered continually, making it a very practical fabric in the home.

Cotton is produced in a huge variety of styles. It can be made into lightweight fabrics such as organza, voile, muslin, lawn, shiny fabric such as furnishing satin, and heavyweight fabrics such as velvet, drills, corduroys, denim, canvas and gabardine, so is extremely versatile for fashion, interior and exterior use.

Cotton is generally mercerized (treated with caustic soda), which gives it a greater affinity for dye colours, but unmercerized cotton can be partly treated with caustic to create a puckered, seer sucker effect (*see* Chapter 7).

TEXTILE INKS AND DYES
- Pigment
- Reactive
- Direct
- Vat
- Multi-purpose dyes
- Discharge printing (pigment discharge yields better results)
- Natural dyes
- Cellulose devoré

LINEN

Linen is made from fibres of the flax plant. Similarly to cotton it is cool, moisture absorbent and can be laundered at high temperatures, and is associated with tablecloths, napkins and bedding.

Its disadvantage as a fashion fabric is its tendency to crease, and linen is also highly expensive, so it is often mixed with cotton.

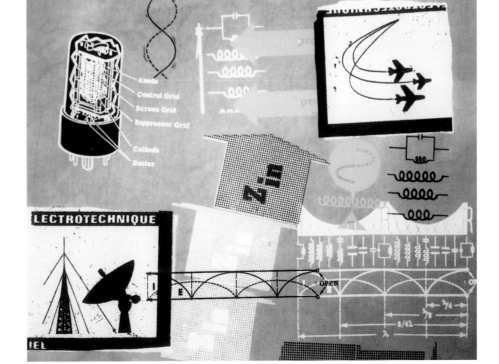

Cotton canvas dyed and printed, by June Fish. (Photograph by June Fish)

TEXTILE INKS AND DYES
- ▨ Pigment
- ▨ Reactive
- ▨ Direct
- ▨ Vat
- ▨ Multi-purpose dyes
- ▨ Discharge printing
- ▨ Natural dyes
- ▨ Cellulose devoré

TEXTILE INKS AND DYES
- ▨ Pigment (only in small quantities as it can upset the surface quality of the fabric)
- ▨ Reactive
- ▨ Acid
- ▨ Direct
- ▨ Multi-purpose dyes
- ▨ Discharge printing
- ▨ Natural dyes

SILK

Silk is obtained from caterpillars or 'silk worms' and has been used as a fabric for thousands of years. It is one of the strongest fabrics, and is a good insulator; many sleeping bags are made from silk. Silk drapes well and is soft on the skin, so it is an ideal fashion fabric. Its high quality of finish makes it the most sophisticated of fabrics and silk is receptive to a wide variety of printing and dyeing effects. Discharge printing, in particular, produces superior results to other fabrics.There are also a huge variety of silks from lightweight organzas, georgettes, habotai, crepes, and heavier raw silks such as doupion and satin.

WOOL

Wool is spun from fleece, and is a highly absorbent fabric and a good insulator. It is mainly used in autumn and winter fashions. It is highly crease resistant and has a degree of elasticity.

Its disadvantages include its lack of strength, which is only approximately one third of the strength of cotton. Wool is more prone to shrinkage and felting than other fabrics after undergoing some of the physical processes connected with dyeing and printing. As an animal fibre, wool requires thorough preparation to remove oils and other impurities before using any patterning processes. It is cheaper than other animal hair fabrics,

Silk fabric delicately hand-printed, by Asahi Ito.

Functional objects for an interior space, printed onto wool, by Natalie Hand.

and is often blended with the more expensive ones such as cashmere to make it (cashmere) more affordable.

TEXTILE INKS AND DYES
- Pigment
- Acid
- Natural dyes
- Multi-purpose dyes
- Protein devoré

VISCOSE RAYON

Viscose was developed in the latter half of the twentieth century, and is a regenerated cellulose polymer. It has similar qualities to cotton, including coolness and absorbency, but has a slightly shinier look. It absorbs dye better than cotton and is colourfast with most inks and dyes, but does not dry as quickly. Its disadvantages are that the fibres are not very strong, especially when wet, and it is highly flammable.

TEXTILE INKS AND DYES
- Pigment
- Reactive
- Direct
- Vat
- Multi-purpose dyes
- Discharge printing
- Cellulose devoré
- Natural dyes

TEXTILE INKS AND DYES
- Pigment
- Acid
- Heat transfer/dispersal papers and inks

POLYAMIDE (NYLON)

Nylon was the first completely synthetic fibre invented, and is now almost entirely made from petroleum products. Its major advantage is its elasticity, and nylon is often used for tights, lingerie and sportswear. For dyeing and printing purposes its advantage over other synthetic fibres is its similarity in chemical make-up to protein fibres which means that the same print and dye products can be used. Brand names for nylon include Tactel.

POLYESTER

Polyester was invented in the 1940s, and is made from petroleum products. It is extremely strong and stable, and can repel water. The downside of this is in its use as a fashion fabric, as it lacks absorbency against perspiration. Modifications are being made all the time and the quality of synthetic fabrics has improved greatly.

Polyester is almost crease-resistant, and is often mixed with cotton for household use, such as bedding. For textile printers and dyers, polyester can be difficult to use as it requires extremely high temperatures to transfer dye. The shape of polyester can be moulded at a high temperature, so permanent creases, pleats and 3D effects can be created (*refer* to Chapter 4).

TEXTILE INKS AND DYES
- Pigment
- Heat transfer/dispersal papers and inks

ACRYLIC FIBRES

Acrylic is a fairly strong, long-lasting and resilient fibre. It can be used in home furnishings and apparel because of its easy care. Carpets, blankets and fleecy fabrics are often made from acrylic fibres. It is preferable to dry clean and avoid exposure to extreme heat. Only a small selection of dyes and inks can be used on acrylic, and basic dyes have a higher health and safety risk than most other dyes, so it may be difficult to use in a home or small workshop environment.

TEXTILE INKS AND DYES
- Pigment
- Basic dyes

MIXED-FIBRE FABRICS

Mixed-fibre fabrics can be integrated with different fibres at the yarn stage, or be knitted or woven together later. Fabrics with mixed fibres can provide difficulties for any surface patterning. If dyeing a polyester/cotton mix, it may be difficult to dye deep colours and fully fix printing inks, as polyester does not respond in the same way as cotton. You may have no choice but to work with a mixed-fibre fabric for reasons including cheaper cost, or its mixed qualities that offer a better overall functional use. You will therefore need to find a compromise for any surface embellishment.

The different qualities of fibres should be worked to your advantage to create exciting dyeing and printing techniques, particularly for devoré printing (*see* Chapter 7). Some fabrics are specifically woven to allow one fibre to be burnt out, creating a sheer patterning effect in the printed areas of the fabric. The most common mixes are: cotton/polyester, silk/viscose, wool/nylon and polyester/metallic yarn. Velvet and satin are widely used as devoré fabrics. The same fibre mixes can also be cross-dyed (*see* Chapter 6), dyeing two separate colours in the same dye bath, by using specific dyes for each fibre.

Polyester fabric, smocked and heat-set, by Sarah Wilson.

Preparation of Fabric for Dyeing and Printing

Most fabrics are sold without any need for pre-scouring for printing and dyeing processes since this is done by the manufacturer. If you are unsure whether the fabric has been treated, then run a few drops of cold water on it. If the water soaks in quickly it is ready to use, if it sits on top then it may need scouring. For dyeing purposes all fabrics will benefit from washing, as soaked fabric will dye more evenly far quicker. Some natural fabrics do contain impurities caused from natural sources, such as oils and wax, or can be caused during the process of making the fabric. If these are not removed then it will provide a resist to any dyeing or printing inks, and lead to an inconsistency in quality. Below are ways of scouring the three main types of fabric.

Cotton. Boil in water containing sodium carbonate, for about 20min (10g of sodium carbonate for 1l water).

Wool. Oil impurities can be removed with an effective neutral detergent in warm water. The most common brand name for detergent is Metapex. Soak the fabric for at least half an hour, and then rinse it out carefully. If the water is too hot it may felt the fabric.

Silk. If you need to remove natural gum from the silk, often caused by residue from the silk worm, wash out the fabric in warm to hot water with soap flakes. Take care not to move the silk from cold to hot water, or the fabric will be damaged.

Fabric Developments

There have been huge developments in fabric technology in the past thirty years, particularly with synthetic fibres. Chapter 4 looked briefly at conductive textiles, where actual functional qualities are being embedded into the fabric, but also huge progress has been attained in the abilities of the fabric itself. If this is an area that is important to your work, you will need to contact the suppliers and companies directly who produce high performance fabrics, as they are unlikely to be found in ordinary retail suppliers. To begin any research look at the products in shops that sell specialist functional textiles such as sportswear shops, clothing for high risk jobs, outdoor equipment and camping shops, and medical suppliers. The Science Museum in London has an informative section on the making and structure of performance fabrics for these types of purposes.

The drawback to overworking these fabrics with print or dye, or reshaping them, is that they may be heavily treated with coatings or finishes on the fabric and it may be impermeable. Inks therefore become unfixable or need to be solvent based. Listed below is a range of fabrics with high-performance qualities.

Composite Fabrics

These are two or more fibres or fabrics that have been joined together to utilize their best properties. These can be applied functionally to fabrics such as trekking clothes, sleeping bags and workwear. Some of these fabrics have natural qualities, and others have been developed for a specific purpose, such as:

Insulation. Wool or polyester made into fleece is an excellent source of insulation, as the method of making fleece traps air, keeping in warmth.

Waterproofing. Fabric has been developed so that a waterproof membrane has been laminated onto an inner fabric; this includes a fabric called Gore-Tex. Another fabric called Permatex can stop water coming through but allows perspiration to be expelled.

Exterior Fabrics

Traditional hard-wearing outdoor fabrics are often too heavy to be carried around, so new developments have produced very lightweight but hard-wearing fabrics such as Paclite. As well as being light, the fabric not only protects against wind chill, but also breathes.

Medical Fabrics

Some materials are now compatible with human tissue, such as those used in implants, or are designed with live cells to aid with recovery from an injury.

Workwear

Most workwear is intended to protect the wearer from contamination, and is also non-linting. This means that it does not shed fibres, important in areas like police work.

Stretch Fabrics

Elastane is a stretch fibre that can extend up to five times its length, helping to create freedom of movement for the wearer. Lycra, a brand name stretch fibre, is often woven or knitted into fabrics to create an overall stretch effect and is used for sportswear in particular.

Non-Woven Fabrics

These fabrics are not made from yarns, but directly from the fibre itself. They can be bonded together in different ways to create extremes of strength, from heavyweight protective fabric to lightweight delicate fabric. Non-wovens are constructed by using adhesives, stitching, felting, needle punching, hydro-entangling (using high-pressure water jets) and thermal bonding (melting fibres together that become rigid when cooled). Their uses vary from tea bags to nappies and operating theatre gowns. Brand names include Tyvek, a fabric used for waterproof overalls, and the light fabric-lining Vilene.

Kingston University (UK) has produced some interesting results with their Re-materialize project, creating a variety of non-woven fabrics made from natural fibres such as jute, cotton, flax, coconut and straw matting. These can be adapted for use in industry. Mixes such as jute and plastic can be heated to melt into a tough fabric used in the car industry.

Standard and specialist pigment ink provide successful results for printing, as well as dry transfer inks and papers for synthetic non-wovens.

Recycled and Environmentally Friendly Fabrics

Recycled second-hand fabrics are fun to source, and can produce unusual and interesting results. High quality fabrics can be found in charity shops, car boot and jumble sales. These are useful if you are on a tight budget, or are looking for something unique, no longer being produced. Overdyeing, printing, embellishing or patchworking already patterned and printed fabrics can create exciting new combinations. Antique fabrics can help provide the mood for a theme or era you are trying to re-create, as part of a student or professional project brief.

Re-using second-hand fabrics is also a good environmental choice, and the textile industry is now seriously looking at ways of improving its record in this area. Fabric manufacturers are much more aware of their responsibility to the environment, and are continually looking for ways to produce biodegradable and non-toxic fabrics, and minimizing dyeing, printing and finishing processes, which are great polluters.

Synthetic materials, despite being thought of as more of an environmental hazard than natural fibres, are leading the way as they can be manipulated at the production stage, cutting out polluting processes later on. Some successful examples include fleece that can now be made from recycled plastic bottles. Experiments have even taken place to grow pre-coloured natural fibres such as cotton to avoid the dyeing stage. Replenishing materials is another key environmental issue. An example of this is the fabric Tencel made from regenerated cellulose.

OPPOSITE PAGE
TOP: **Non-woven material over-printed with discharge ink, by Hannah Sessions.**

BOTTOM: **Printing onto recycled fabrics, by Malin Svard. (Photograph by June Fish)**

The wood pulp is taken from forests that are specifically maintained and replenished. The fair and safe working conditions and salaries for textile workers is another environmental issue that is now being addressed.

Labelling and Care of Fabrics

If you are a designer maker and intend to sell your patterned fabrics for a functional use such as clothing or interior textiles, then it is important to label your fabrics for washing and general aftercare.

Most fabrics need care over washing treatments. Look around retail fashion and homeware shops and check how certain fabrics for particular functions have been labelled for wash temperature, drying, ironing and even storage. The main fabrics that have washing concerns include: wool as it is prone to shrinkage and felting in hot water conditions; acrylic fibres can stretch out of shape when not washed carefully; and acetate should preferably be dry cleaned, to prevent possible creasing and cracking from washing. Ironing is also a potential problem and can cause shininess on synthetics.

For interior fabrics you may be required to fireproof any finished pieces, particularly if they are in a public setting such as a restaurant or office interior. Fireproofing substances can usually be bought from art and design shops, particularly canvas specialists. Any flammable wadding or padding will need to be labelled as a potential fire hazard.

If your textile piece is intended for exterior use, it is probably worth considering waterproof fabrics at the start. Sailing shops sell useful sturdy materials. If this is not possible then you can apply a waterproof coating afterwards in liquid form, that can be sprayed on.

Any print or dye techniques you have used, will certainly affect washing instructions. *See* Chapter 6 for aftercare of dyed fabrics.

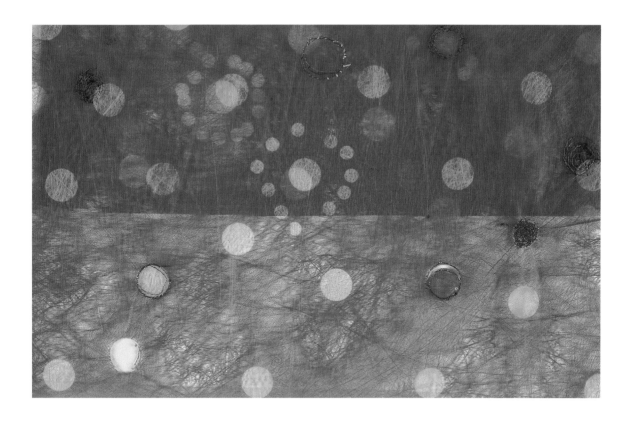

REG 33   <u>CYCLAMEN</u>   REG 33

8 oz Reducer   1 oz Lemon
1 oz Helio   1/4 oz Astra P.
3/4 oz Rhodamine

CAMPION PINK   SEE P.

275   <u>CELESTIAL DIRT</u>   275

1/2 g Saffl
1/2 g Auramine
5 1/4 g Meth Blue
45 g Reducer

<u>CLARET</u>

Reg. 295

8 oz Rhodamine
2 oz Helio
1 oz Auramine
1 oz Basic
1 oz Meth.

Reg: 295

5 4   <u>Chestnut Brown</u>   5 4
2 1/2 Auramine   1/2 meth   blue
1 Helio 5   1   Trg.
1 Rhodamine

1/16 g

1/16 g <u>CATHLEEN'S PINK</u>

16   Reducer
1/16 Astra Phloxine
R

CHAPTER 6

COLOURING AND PATTERNING WITH DYES AND DYE RECIPES

IMPORTANT NOTE: The recipes and materials in the following chapters are potentially hazardous. It is important that you are aware of any risks or hazards to your health. Please read the Health and Safety section (*see* pp. 149–50) before using these recipes.

This chapter will look at ways of utilizing dyeing, to produce exciting options with colour and innovative ways of creating pattern without the use of printing methods. Dyeing techniques, including tie-dyeing and resist dyeing, are still widely used in fashion and textiles today. Some very ancient processes can easily create patterns such as stripes, geometrics, circles and abstract painterly patterns. This can be a useful option if you are short of printing space or silk-screen equipment, and need a quick and convenient solution. The patterns created with dyeing techniques also have a softer more blended look on your fabric, instead of the sharp edges achieved through silk-screen printing. It adds another dimension and style to your patterning, and can be combined successfully with overprinting and painting methods. The results can be unpredictable, but this can lead to exciting unexpected discoveries.

To ensure that you obtain the best permanent results possible, this chapter will provide in-depth practical information on dye types, dye recipes and fixatives. Dyes range from synthetically made powders or liquids that are in general use today, through to natural dyes. Although these latter have decreased in use, they are still valuable particularly with the increasing concern about environmental issues. If you are hoping to sell hand-dyed products, then the fixatives and methods of dyeing to aid resistance and colourfastness to the dye when in functional use, are hugely important to your customer. I am sure we can all think of instances when fabric has washed badly, or dye has rubbed off from furnishings and clothing, or faded in sunlight. All these issues need to be resolved in advance, through experiment and sampling.

Dyeing can also enhance a fabric, for example, dyed velvet reflects colours differently in light, and fabrics made with different fibre mixes, such as polyester and cotton, can dye separate colours, on the same piece of fabric. Using a dyed ground is a great way of getting started if you are daunted by working on blank, uncoloured fabric, and more practical for functional fabrics, such as furnishings that become dirty more easily when they are white or lightly coloured.

In order to achieve the best results, it is preferable (and easier) to use natural fabrics with these dyeing techniques. Dyes are also available for synthetic fabrics but some of the dye carriers and fixatives are extremely pungent, and it is not advisable to use them in a poorly ventilated area. The dry transfer method also mentioned in Chapters 3 and 7 is a safer alternative, but a recipe for dyeing synthetic fabrics will be included in this chapter. Keep referring back to the previous chapter on fabric types and qualities to help you with your choices. Fabric dyes can also be used quite easily on paper (*see* Chapter 3) to complement your fabric work and provide an alternative to paint colours.

Dye notebook from the 1930s belonging to Joyce Clissold. (Central St Martins Museum and Study Collection)

Dyeing Techniques

Before starting I strongly advise you to read the section on health and safety (*see* pp.149–50), and consult your supplier on the least hazardous dyes available to buy. You will also need to equip yourself with useful materials (*see* box).

If you are a novice, before plunging in to dye your main pieces, always test your colours first and keep an accurate record of your results, which will prove invaluable for future use.

Testing is important because dyes can react slightly differently on different fabrics and a variation in dyeing times changes the shade of the colour. Your budget may be limited so you will want to obtain as many colour combinations as possible from a handful of dyes, and you will find a few that do not mix well together (for mixing dye colours, *refer* to the section on colour theory in Chapter 2).

Although the actual recipes for dyeing are straightforward, your initial attempts may produce patchy and unfixed colours, because of a lack of experience and understanding in controlling the colour take-up. Before trying out experimental techniques, dye a sample fabric in one even colour so that you have understood the process and relationship between fabric and dye. Listed below are a range of dyeing terms and techniques, starting off with the most straightforward, and gradually moving towards more complex patterning techniques. Remember to cross reference these techniques with the guidelines for dyeing and dyeing recipes listed further on in this chapter.

Piece Dyeing: is the dyeing of one type of material or yarn, such as a 100 per cent cotton, into one single even colour. This involves the fabric being completely submerged into a dye bath.

Over-Dyeing: is fully or partially dyeing a fabric that has already been initially dyed. Your final colour will be affected by the original base colour, so refer to the section on colour theory, to establish the overall colour possibilities.

Union Dyeing: is achieving a single even colour on a fabric or yarn made from different fibre combinations such as wool and cotton. To accomplish this, you will need to use appropriate types of dye for each fibre, matching the colour, to try and achieve an overall single colour effect.

Cross Dyeing: a contrasting colour effect achieved by dyeing more than one colour on a fabric or yarn made from different fibre mixes, such as cotton and polyester. Use the appropriate dye for each fibre type; the dyes can be put into one dye bath, if they dye at the same temperature, or dyed separately. Some suppliers sell dye products for this particular process including the Alter Ego range from Fibrecraft. The contrast is more difficult to achieve on natural fabric combinations, but more obvious on a

synthetic and natural mix. Cross-check with Chapter 5 on fabrics and what dye products are most suitable. Even though wool and nylon are natural and synthetic respectively, they still both dye with acid dyes, so the contrast will be less visible. The results of cross dyeing particularly stand out on fabrics woven and knitted

---

EQUIPMENT FOR DYEING FABRICS

- ■ Dust mask, rubber gloves and overalls (and work in a well-ventilated area when mixing dyes and auxiliaries – avoid using a kitchen area)

- ■ A small set of scales; for weighing dyes and fixatives

- ■ Metal spoons and metal jugs

- ■ A portable electric stove

- ■ Metal vessels of various sizes (hot-water dyeing)

- ■ Plastic bowls (cold-water dyeing)

- ■ Sink for washing out

- ■ A washing machine or spin dryer for final rinses

Materials for resist techniques:

- ■ String

- ■ Wood cut into different shapes

- ■ Clamps

- ■ Rolling pin

- ■ Syringes or pipettes

- ■ Plastic bags

- ■ Needle and thread

- ■ Staple gun

- ■ Pegs or bulldog clips

- ■ Paintbrushes

- ■ Notebook to keep a record of your results

for devoré purposes (*see* Chapter 7), when one fibre type is completely burnt out in areas, leaving the other exposed.

Ombre Dyeing: is a dyeing effect that graduates the fabric colour from light to dark. This is achieved by lowering the fabric or yarn in the dye vat in gradual stages. If you work from dry fabric and lower the fabric into your dye bath at regular intervals (for example every ten minutes) you will get clear definitions in the changes of colour shading. The best results are when the colour changes are less pronounced and more blended. To achieve this, wet the fabric first, and immerse the fabric at more frequent rates into the dye bath. If you dye the fabric an overall base colour to begin with, this will also make the different shades blend in more (an Ombre effect can also be achieved by using printing methods).

Dip Dyeing: this is a multi-coloured dye effect, created by carefully dipping sections of your yarn or fabric into different colour dye baths. A stripy effect can be achieved by keeping the colours separated as much as possible. Do this by placing plastic bags over the areas you wish to keep from dyeing a particular colour, and tie them tightly with string or a rubber band. This will prevent dye migrating to other areas, and also reduce the risk of accidentally picking up unwanted dye patches. Firstly, prepare the required number of dye baths, and keep them close together to avoid dripping dye over the work surface, which could accidentally stain your fabric. Make sure you are wearing gloves, as you will be continually handling the fabric. Dip the fabric in each dye bath until you are satisfied with the colour. To keep each colour as pure as possible, you may have to wash excessive dye

Dip-dyeing fabric in two different colour dye baths.

out of the fabric, before dipping it into the next colour. Keep the other sections of fabric protected in plastic, while you are washing out the dyed areas, to prevent any staining. If you want to blend in the colours more, dip the fabric randomly without using plastic, to allow the dye to spread. When washing the fabric out, try and lay the fabric as flat as possible in a sink or a bath, to prevent different dye colours from migrating more than necessary to other areas.

Space Dyeing: this creates a random multi-coloured pattern effect, by painting or injecting different colour dyes directly onto fabric. The fabric should be washed, and while still wet, folded and rolled up, then tied with string into a bundle. Place the fabric in a plastic bowl and paint or inject dye through syringes or pipettes. This may be done randomly or in a certain sequence. Rinse the fabric out to remove excess dye, laying the fabric as flat as possible in a sink or bath to stop the dye contaminating other areas.

If you intend to overprint or pattern your fabric after dyeing, then it is probably worth keeping your colour palette pale or tonal, as a busy, multicoloured background effect will absorb any painting or printing on top.

Resist Dyeing

Resist dyeing is a controlled way of tying, clamping, or painting wax on areas of fabric, to create a resist to repeated layers of dye colours, forming negative patterns. Resist techniques work particularly well if you continually over-dye the fabric from light colours through to dark colours, while continually reapplying wax or retying different sections of the fabric, so that layers of different colour patterns emerge. If you do not wish any of the fabric to remain white, then it is a good idea to dye your fabric a base colour first before starting to apply resist methods. Always start from the lightest colour in your palette and gradually build up to darker shades, after you apply each method of resist. Tie-dyeing is a traditional and common method of resist dyeing, and many examples can be seen in African and Asian textiles (*see* Chapter 2). A specialized form of tying, pleating and stitch resists is called Shibori.

Shibori

Shibori originated from ancient Japan, and still has a high profile today partly due to its use in modern Japanese fashion and textile design in combination with innovations in fabric technology

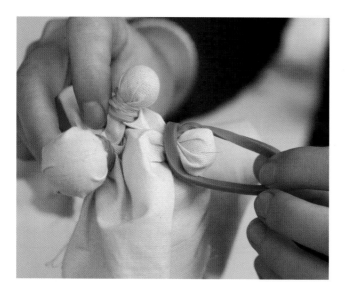

**Tying in marbles with elastic bands
to create circular resist patterns.**

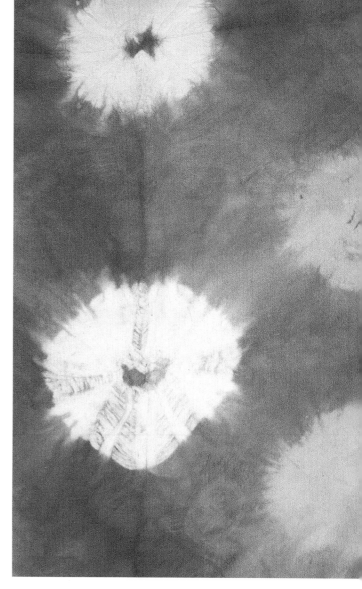

Overdyed fabric sample with resisted circular ring effect.

(*see* Chapter 4). Shibori methods range from simple resist techniques through to highly skilled processes that will require a more specialized book on the topic, and plenty of experience. Below are a range of basic methods for some straightforward and easily achievable resist dye effects.

To create ring or circular resist effects, gather small sections of the fabric together, randomly or in a regular sequence, and wrap the gathered areas tightly with string until they are completely tied and covered up (or for finer areas, use thread). After dyeing the fabric, the string can be removed to leave resisted ring shapes, or leave the string tied in and add more tied areas after the first dye colour, and then overdye the fabric. Repeating this process will build up layers of colour rings.

To create a uniform resist effect, the fabric can be folded repeatedly into triangular shapes until it is quite small, and then one point of the fabric triangle tied with string, giving a regular ring-shaped pattern all over in sequence.

Varieties of resist shapes such as dots and diamonds can be achieved by using this method, if the fabric is gathered and tied in different ways. Small objects that alter the shapes, such as dried beans, can also be tied in.

To create geometric forms with dye, fold the fabric into squares, triangles and pleats of different lengths and widths. Collect some flat pieces of wood cut to different sizes and shapes,

always making sure that there are two pieces of wood exactly the same shape and size. Sandwich the folded fabric between the two pieces, allowing some of the fabric to be exposed. Then place a G clamp tightly around the wood, and tie a long piece of string to the clamp, so that you can retrieve it from your dye bath as it will need to be completely submerged. After dyeing, repeat the process folding the fabric in a different way.

For pleats fold the fabric in a concertina style, and then sandwich the fabric in between two pieces of long thin wood, with the fabric's edges exposed. This will create dyed lines on your fabric, and if you refold the fabric the opposite way you can create a grid pattern.

To produce straight or wavy resisted lines on the fabric, you will need a pole such as a rolling pin or tubing, and some string. Wrap your fabric around the pole (the more times it is wrapped around, the less the effect will be on the inner portion of fabric). Then wrap string continually around on top of the fabric; if this is done randomly the resisted areas will be wavy lines, if it is uniform wrapping, the lines will be straight.

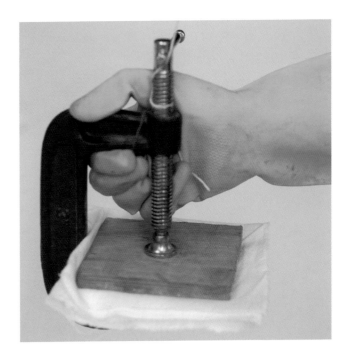

Fabric folded into squares, and clamped tightly in order to create a resisted geometric effect.

BELOW: **Overdyed fabric, after being clamped between wood blocks several times.**

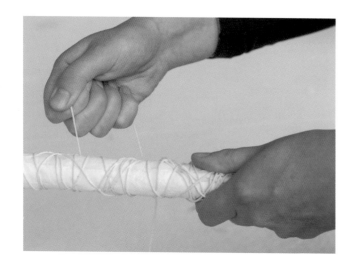

Wrapping fabric around a pole, and tying randomly around with string.

BELOW: **Result of resisted string effect after being wrapped around a pole.**

Once tied in with string the fabric can also be pushed and condensed together to enhance the resist. For different effects the fabric can also be twisted around itself or stitched before being wrapped around the pole.

Stitching can also create interesting resists. Firstly, sew large tacking stitches in lines across the fabric; nylon or polyester thread is useful, as it will be resistant to the dye for natural fabrics. Gather the thread ends and hold them taut, at the same time pushing the fabric together to gather it. Then dye the fabric.

A more elaborate use of stitching can create additional resisted effects and patterns, such as wavy and circular stitching and smocked patterns. Wash any excess dye out of the fabric before removing the thread.

To create a resisted cracked dye effect (similar to the effects of cracked wax) you can use a finger pleating technique. Wetting the fabric first will make it easier to manipulate. Lay it flat on a work surface, and gather it together with your fingers, eventually packing the fabric tightly together. Tie the fabric bundle up with string, and drop into your dye bath.

Hand-gathering fabric together for a resist dye effect.

Once gathered, tie tightly with string and then dye.

BELOW: **The resulting effect is similar to cracked wax.**

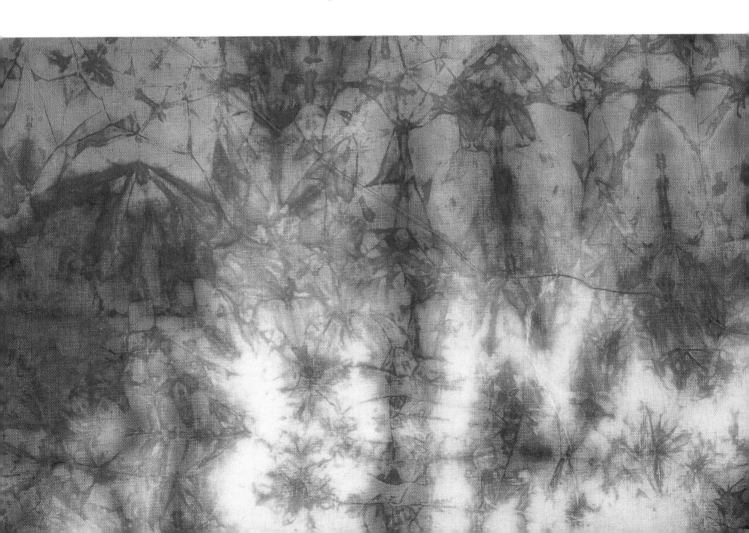

All these techniques can be combined on one piece of fabric, so be experimental, and maximize your potential for patterning options. Also the resists can work in reverse, where you start with a pre-dyed colour, apply your form of resist, and bleach or discharge out your dye, leaving the resist as a positive colour image, while the fabric generally returns to white.

Shibori resist techniques are also used to mould the shape of synthetic fabric into 3D shapes by heat-setting the fabric (*refer* to Chapter 4 for details).

Batik and Wax Resist

Batik and wax resist are traditional methods of patterning fabric, and examples can be traced back to ancient China, seventeenth- and eighteenth-century India, Peru and the Middle East. Indonesia, particularly Java, is probably the best known producer of batik.

Wax resists work best on cotton and silk, but it is worth experimenting on different fabrics. To create clearer definition when drawing with wax, stretch the fabric over a wooden frame, and pin or staple it around the edges as taut as possible. For small areas an embroidery ring will be suitable. If wax is applied to a fabric unstretched or directly against a table surface it will stick to the table behind and the wax pattern will spread and blur.

The wax is usually purchased in granules and will need to be heated in a metal bowl to keep it in liquid form while you are using it. The safest vessel to use is an electric wax pot that maintains the correct temperature.

There are different types of wax that offer different qualities including:

Paraffin wax: is more brittle and can give a more cracked effect.

Beeswax: is softer and more pliable, and less likely to break off.

The tool most widely used to apply wax is called a tjanting. This has a wooden handle with a small copper bowl and a funnel attached to the end. The bowl is used to scoop up the wax and then you draw with it while it pours out of the funnel. This method takes a bit of practice, as the wax solidifies quickly, and the pressure applied on the fabric can result in too much wax coming out of the funnel. Have an old cloth on hand to soak up any free-flowing wax.

Plan out your design in advance lightly in pencil, as the batik process is bold and spontaneous, and you will need to

be quick and positive with your wax drawing. Tjantings come in different sizes, so if you are finding it difficult to produce lines or intricate drawing, it may be worth investing in a tjanting with a slimmer funnel. For bolder textural mark-making, apply the wax directly to your fabric with heat-resistant brushes – stiff bristled brushes such as hogshair are better. For all-over effects, such as a cracked effect, dip the fabric in the melted wax and, when it has solidified, crush the fabric, allowing some of the wax to fall off. Once this has been dyed and the wax completely removed, it will have created a cracked dye effect.

When you are applying the wax ensure that it has soaked through to the back of the fabric or it will not resist the dye completely. The wax solidifies quickly, depending on how thickly you have applied it. Once solid, dyeing can now take place, by

Using a tjanting to apply wax in a controlled manner.

Covering the fabric entirely with wax, and scrunching it together to create a cracked dye effect.

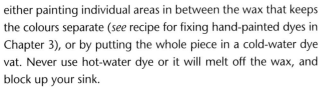

Alternatively use a brush for bolder wax marks.

either painting individual areas in between the wax that keeps the colours separate (*see* recipe for fixing hand-painted dyes in Chapter 3), or by putting the whole piece in a cold-water dye vat. Never use hot-water dye or it will melt off the wax, and block up your sink.

To build up layers of colour patterns, you will need to dye, wash out the fabric and dry it off before adding another layer of wax pattern to partially protect the first dye colour. This process should be repeated each time.

Once you have completely finished the dyeing process or want to start removing the wax, place the fabric in the middle of some newspapers or newsprint, and with a hot iron melt the wax so that it absorbs into the paper. Once you are satisfied that this method is exhausted, wash the fabric in warm water with detergent, which will help to soften it.

Gutta is not a wax, but a paste that is usually used for drawing images for silk painting, and keeps the painted dye colours separate. You will need a gutta outliner for drawing, and water-based gutta can be washed out of the fabric.

Cracked wax effect during dyeing.

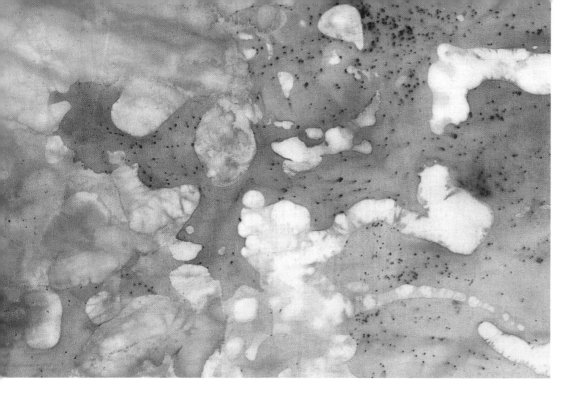

Painted wax resist, left to soak in rusty filings, to create a rust-colour effect.

BELOW: **Range of synthetic dyes in the dye lab at Central St Martins Art College.**

Dye Types and Recipes

Natural dye products were used until the discovery of synthetically made dyes in the nineteenth century, by William Perkin. The first of these were basic dyes, now mainly used just for acrylic fibres, followed by acid and direct dyes for protein and cellulose fibres. These quickly replaced the natural dyes that offered more unpredictable results, but were less vibrant and colourfast. This was followed in the 1950s by the development of reactive dyes by ICI, also for natural fibres. The discovery of all these dye products revolutionized the textile printing industry, and they are still the standard dyes used today.

There are various brand names for each type of dye, and each supplier may sell a different brand, so when purchasing dyes ask for the dye type – that is, direct, acid, reactive and so on rather than a brand name.

Many of the dye colours will be labelled with their colour, followed by a letter, number or percentage written on them. This can sometimes give an indication to the fastness or solubility of the dye, or can tell you if a colour leans towards another colour – for example, a violet labelled with an R, may mean it is a red/violet. Percentages may indicate dyes that are a different strength from the usual standard. Your supplier will be able to help you with this.

Most of the dyes can also be used to create colour print pastes on the same type of fabric, so cross-reference with the section on print recipes to find the best dyes for working in

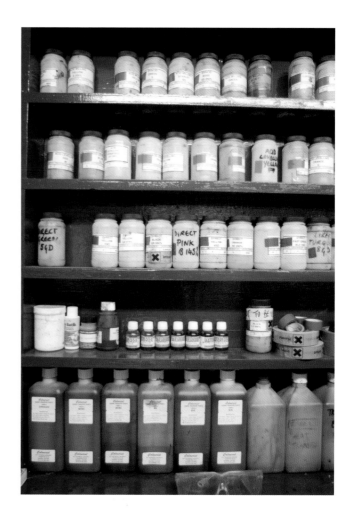

both dye and print, to make purchasing materials more economical. It is unnecessary to buy a huge range of colours, because once you are more experienced at colour mixing, six to eight colours will be enough.

Reactives

Reactive dyes work on all cellulose fibres and silk. They offer excellent wash fastness, a wide range of bright colours and will dye at low temperatures. Many other dye types require hot water, so if you are unable to access a stove, then cold-water dyes are the obvious choice. Dylon produces a range of cold-water dyes that can easily be purchased.

The main brand name for reactives is PROCION, and the most versatile range for dyeing is the MX range. If you can access hot-water dye facilities, manufacturers recommend the H-E hot-water range for denser woven fabrics.

The disadvantage of reactives is that they can carry a higher health risk than direct dyes that can also be used to dye the same category of fibre. Seek advice from your supplier, who will be able to provide you with health and safety data on each dye colour, so you can avoid the more hazardous colours (*see* boxes, p.112).

Direct Dyes

Direct dyes were superseded by reactives, because of their inferior wash fastness and their inability to dye colours as brightly as reactives, but they are still useful on cellulose fabrics and generally carry a lower health risk. Directs are economical but require hot water for their application, so you will need a stove and stainless steel saucepans, or a small Burco boiler for dyeing in (*see* box, p.113).

Acid Dyes

Acid dyes are used for dyeing protein fibres, and also work well on polyamide (nylon) that has a similar chemical make up to protein fibres. Acids produce a good range of bright colours with excellent qualities for wash fastness, and are divided into different types, the two main ones being listed on p.113. Like direct dyes they require hot water temperatures, and care needs to be taken with silk and wool that can felt when overheated (*see* box, p.113).

GENERAL GUIDELINES FOR DYEING

Weighing the fabric should be the first thing you do, as the quantities of dye and fixatives for each dye recipe are calculated by the dry weight of the fabric you are dyeing. Then wash the fabric thoroughly (*see* Chapter 5 for scouring fabrics).

If you wish to mix two or more colours together, make sure that the dye quantity does not exceed the total amount necessary for dyeing your fabric.

All the dye powder should be dissolved prior to being added to the dye bath, generally in hot water. Never add concentrated or undissolved dye directly onto your fabric in the dye bath.

There is no exact set time for how long you should keep your fabric in the dye bath. This entirely depends on the type of fabric and the strength of the dye (some vary), and when you feel satisfied that you have achieved your colour. A guideline would be approximately one hour for a full shade of colour.

Remember the fabric always dries a shade lighter than it looks when wet. For pale shades, use less dye and fixatives rather than putting your fabric in a full-strength dye bath for less time. Doing this may result in patchy dyeing, and is also a waste of dye and chemicals that then need to be disposed of.

Once your fabric is in the dye bath, keep it moving regularly to ensure an even dye distribution.

With hot water dyes, never allow them to boil over, as this can affect the quality of the fabric, and always immerse the fabric in the dye bath before it has heated up, or the dye take-up will be too quick and lead to uneven dyeing.

In hard water areas Calgon may need to be added into the dye bath to soften the water.

Do not dry the dyed fabric directly on surfaces such as radiators, or they will dry unevenly. Try and air-hang the fabric to dry, preferably after spindrying.

Hand-painted dyes may require extra fixation (*see* Chapter 3).

PROCION MX (COLD/WARM WATER DYEING)

Weight of fabric 100g

Full shade of colour:

- 4g dye
- 100g salt (sodium chloride)
- 10g soda ash
- 3l warm water (40°C)

1) For medium or pale shades reduce all the quantities of dye and chemicals in proportion – do not reduce the volume of water.

2) After pre-washing your fabric (*see* Chapter 5), fill a bowl (plastic will do) with the required amount of water, add Calgon if in a hard-water area.

3) Weigh out and dissolve the dye powder separately in hot water (wear a dusk mask at this point) and then add the dissolved dye to the dye bath.

4) Weigh out the salt and add to the dye bath, and stir to dissolve it.

5) Immerse the fabric and stir for a few minutes to ensure the even distribution of dye on the fabric.

6) Half-way through dyeing, add the dissolved soda ash (remove the fabric briefly while you are doing this) and this will aid with fixation of the dye to fabric.

7) Sporadically stir the fabric.

8) Once you are satisfied with the colour, remove the fabric and wash out any excess dye in warm water until it runs clear.

9) Particularly with heavy shades, the fabric will need washing in hot water with a detergent such as Metapex to clear excess dye.

10) As MX dyes are cold-water dyes, they are ideal for any wax resist pastes that would melt off with all the other hot-water dyes.

PROCION H-E (HOT-WATER DYES)

Weight of fabric 100g

Full shade of colour:

- 4g dye
- 100g salt (sodium chloride)
- 10g soda ash
- 3l cold water

1) For medium to pale shades, reduce all the quantities of dye and chemicals in proportion – do not reduce the volume of water.

2) After pre-washing your fabric (*see* Chapter 5), fill your dye bath (made of stainless steel, as other metals may affect the colour) with warm water. Add Calgon if in a hard-water area.

3) Weigh out and dissolve the dye in a separate metal container in warm/hot water (wear a dust mask), then add to the dye bath.

4) Weigh the salt and add to the dye bath, and stir to dissolve it.

5) Immerse the fabric and stir for a few minutes. At the same time, begin to raise the temperature of the dye bath to around 80°C (steam should begin to rise off the surface). Use a wooden implement to stir the fabric, until it reaches this temperature over a period of 10 to 15min. You will then need to maintain this temperature for at least half an hour.

6) Weigh out and dissolve the soda ash in hot water and add to the dye bath. You will need to remove the fabric briefly. Stir the fabric occasionally for around 20min, maintaining the hot temperature.

7) When satisfied with the colour, remove the fabric and wash in warm water until it runs clear.

With heavy shades particularly, the fabric will need washing in hot water in a detergent such as Metapex to remove excess dye.

DIRECT DYES

Weight of fabric 100g

Full shade of colour:

- 4g of dye

- 20g salt (sodium chloride)

- 3l hot water (80–90°C)

1) For medium to pale shades reduce all the quantities of dye and chemicals in proportion – do not alter the volume of water.

2) Weigh out and dissolve the dye in a separate container in hot water (wear a dust mask).

3) Fill your dye bath with warm water and add the dye and a third of a portion of the salt. Then add your pre-washed fabric and stir.

4) Slowly begin to heat the water to the required temperature. If you raise the temperature too quickly the dye will take to the fabric immediately and may be patchy due to the lack of immersion time.

5) After 10min, add another portion of salt, followed 10min later by the last portion (you will need to remove the fabric) and bring the dye bath up to the correct temperature.

6) When you are satisfied with the colour, remove the fabric and wash out in cold water, followed by detergent in hot water.

ACID DYES

Weight of fabric 100g

Full shade of colour:

- 4g of dye

- 5ml acetic acid (at 20 per cent strength)

- 20g sodium sulphate (Glauber's salt)

- 3l hot water (80–100°C)

1) For medium to pale shades reduce all the quantities of dye and chemicals in proportion – do not alter the volume of water.

2) Wash the fabric thoroughly (*see* Chapter 5).

3) Soak the fabric in the required amount of water for your dye bath with the acetic acid and Glauber's salt, for approximately 15min, so that the fabric absorbs the fixatives.

4) Dissolve the dye in a separate container of hot water (wear a dust mask), and then add into the dye bath after 15min. Remove the fabric first if it is already in the dye bath.

5) Slowly heat up the dye bath, but do not reach boiling point. Once the bath is beginning to produce steam maintain that temperature for around 20 or 30min, then turn off the heat source, allowing the bath to cool down for another 20min.

6) These times may vary according to the depth of colour you want. Once you are satisfied with the colour, rinse out the fabric in warm water until it runs clear, and then in hot water with a little detergent. Wool can felt if moved directly from hot to cold water, so maintain a warm washing temperature.

Acid levelling dyes. Levelling or equalizing dyes penetrate the fibre easily and work particularly well on wool and nylon. They dye the fabric more evenly, and are the easiest to control, but do not have a high degree of wash fastness.

Acid milling dyes. Milling dyes have a better degree of wash fastness, but do not dye as evenly as levelling dyes (*see* box, *above*).

Vat Dyes

Vat dyes have an exceptionally high quality for wash fastness and light fastness, so are used in industry frequently, but are difficult to use outside this environment because of the specific conditions needed for successful results. They are not recommended for use in the home or workshop environment for this reason, and because of some of the hazardous chemicals involved. One colour and recipe that is extremely popular with textile dyers is indigo dyeing, which originates from traditional Asian resist dyeing and printing techniques (*see* Chapter 1). The deep blue it creates also became an important colour in English textiles and ceramics called 'China Blue'. Indigo is most often used to dye denim.

Vat dyes work best on cellulose fibres, but are insoluble in water unless they are treated with an alkaline reducing agent. The colour does not appear until oxidation in air. The recipe below is for synthetic indigo, a natural recipe for indigo can also be found in specialized natural dye books. The results will be the same, and work on all natural fabrics.

INDIGO DYEING RECIPE

For sample amounts of fabric:

- 15g of indigo vat grains
- 15g caustic soda
- 10g sodium hydrosulphite
- 5l warm water

1) Firstly make sure you are wearing heavy duty rubber gloves, eye protection, dust mask and an apron, and have *heatproof pots* (a heatproof glass jar with a tight-fitting lid is most suitable). Some of the chemicals are corrosive so you will need to take great care; if you are working at home, it may be more suitable to work outside.

2) If you are intending to make a large vat, then you weigh out and mix the chemicals first in a smaller jar, and add the mixture to a larger tub with the full amount of warm water for the recipe.

3) Add the caustic soda to a small quantity of cold water in a strong plastic pot, and use a wooden stirrer to dissolve the caustic. This will immediately heat up.

4) Using a heatproof glass jar, weigh out and add the indigo vat grains, and enough warm water to disperse the grains.

5) Follow on by adding the caustic soda solution and sodium hydrosulphite, and then put a tight-fitting lid on, preventing air getting to the mixture.

6) Fill either a larger stainless steel or tough plastic tub with the remainder of the warm water, and add the indigo stock. Make sure it has a tight-fitting lid, and leave for one hour. If possible, the tub should be placed in a larger vessel or sink of warm water to keep the temperature constant.

7) When the solution is completely dissolved, it should look yellow in colour.

8) Pre-wash your fabric and then remove the lid and add the fabric to the solution. Make sure you put the lid back on immediately, and leave your fabric in the vat for approximately 2min. Agitate the tub, to ensure the fabric is being immersed in the dye.

9) Remove the fabric, allowing excess dye to drop back into the vat.

10) Air hang the fabric, its exposure to air will gradually make it turn blue. Once the colour has oxidized, wash out the fabric, and if the colour has faded, repeat the dyeing process.

This process can be repeated continually until you achieve the shade of blue you are satisfied with.

11) Wash the excess dye out of the fabric in cold water, and then in warm water with detergent. The vat of indigo should be reusable for several days, with the lid kept on at all times.

Disperse Dyes

DRY TRANSFER METHOD

Dispersal dyes were invented to overcome the problem of synthetically made fabrics, particularly acetate, that are hydrophobic or water repellent. The invention of polyester expanded the usage of dyes, as dispersal dye is suitable for all synthetic fibres.

The dry method of applying dispersal dyes to fabric is the safest, and most successful, as it can reach the higher temperatures needed to achieve bright colours (see Chapter 3 for creative ways of applying heat transfer to synthetic fabrics).

The dye can be bought in liquid form, sometimes known as heat transfer inks, which, for health and safety purposes, are better to purchase than the dyes in powder form. The only disadvantage of the liquid colours is that they can dry out in the bottom of the tub if not used regularly, so keep them well shaken and don't buy a huge quantity in advance.

The dye colour can be transferred by firstly sponging or painting the dye onto paper (newsprint is sufficient, but can slightly warp giving an uneven effect). Once the ink is dry, place the paper face down onto the fabric and iron at the temperatures listed below for each type of fabric. Never allow the heat source to have direct contact with the fabric or it will risk melting it. Clean paper or protective cloth in between the heat source and fabric will prevent this, and help keep the equipment and fabric clean from dye stains.

Polyester – 220°C for 30sec
Nylon – 200°C for 30sec
Cellulose acetate – 200°C for 20sec

If you have access to a heat transfer press, the application will be more even and is much quicker to apply to large pieces of fabric. It is worth investing in one if this is going to become central to your work.

Natural Dyes

Natural dyes have traditionally been the main source of colour for fabrics since ancient times. Despite their decline in use in industry, natural dyes still have a niche market today. They can be subdivided into different categories: plant and vegetable dyes, insect dyes, and mineral dyes, cochineal being the best known insect-based dye, and red ochre, a mineral dye. Natural dyes work on all natural fabrics, but not synthetics, and produce a rich, versatile colour range that is easily achievable.

DISPERSAL DYEING

A dye bath can be made for full immersion dyeing of synthetic fabrics and some plastics. Polyester will only be able to be dyed pale to medium shades with immersion dyeing.

Weight of fabric 100g

Full shade of colour:

- 4g dye
- 3g dispersing agent
- 3l hot water 90–100°C

1) After pre-washing your fabric, put the required amount of water into a heatproof vessel, preferably stainless steel.

2) Weigh out the dye (wear a dust mask) into a separate jug with warm water, reducing the quantities of dye and dispersing agent if you require paler shades.

3) Add Calgon in hard water areas, and then add the dissolved dye to the dye bath with the dispersing agent. Only use dispersing agent if you have good ventilation; you will be able to achieve a certain level of colour without it.

4) Immerse the fabric while the dye bath is warm, and gradually heat up. Stir the fabric until the required temperature is reached, which is almost boiling point. Maintain this temperature for about 20min, then allow the temperature to drop, before washing out your fabric in warm water when you are satisfied with the colour.

The downside of natural dyes is the inconsistency of the colour, because of the difficulty in getting equally matched colour from natural products, so one batch may look slightly different from another. Also colours fade easier, and dyes are not as applicable for printing with as with their synthetic counterparts. It can also be difficult to obtain large enough amounts

CHAPTER 7

PRINTING PROCESSES AND PRINT RECIPES

Silk-Screen Printing

Screen-printing transformed the application of surface pattern on fabrics in the twentieth century, beginning with manual printing methods, through to today's automated print equipment mainly used in industry. The future role of screen printing is unclear as digital printing technology gains more and more momentum, but manual methods are still used for sampling, and producing print patterns on small runs on fabric and paper, and are ideal for textile print designers.

The disadvantage for designers working at home or in a small studio is accessing certain facilities, particularly a deep enough wash-out area for chemically cleaning and washing the screen, and an exposure unit for making water-resistant photostencil patterns on the screen. There are alternative ways of using silk screen without screen exposure (*see* Chapter 3). But, for example, if you need to produce a large number of the same images such as multiple T-shirt prints, then processing the screen with light-sensitive emulsion will definitely be longer lasting, as many other methods only produce one-off prints. Silk screens come in various shapes and sizes, including sample size, dress width and furnishing width. Some are fitted with bars and bolts necessary for registering a repeat image (*see* Chapter 2). Even if you are producing large-scale repeats and images, it is always worth having sample screens to test your colours and inks first.

Hand-printed motifs onto silk with acid print paste, then stitched and quilted together, by Jaewon Kim.

Preparing a Silk Screen

Screen Mesh

Despite being called a silk screen, most screens are now made of polyester filament, which is generally resistant to the effects of the textile printing materials you will be using. The mesh comes in various hole sizes; the wider the polyester weave in the mesh, the more ink that will be pushed through onto your fabric. Before buying check with your supplier what their recommendation is for mesh sizes when printing on fabric. The mesh is usually more coarse on screens being printed on fabric than those for paper that absorb less ink, so needs a tighter mesh to prevent as much ink coming through. Below is a guideline to screen mesh size.

SCREEN MESH SIZE	
Fabric threads number per centimetre	*Type of printing*
36T	Heavyweight fabric / thick printing inks
43T	General textiles
48T	General textiles to lighter weight fabrics
77T	Lighter weight fabrics

It should be possible to be re-expose and reuse the mesh for printing several times. Its longevity often depends on how quickly and how well you clean it after printing. A hot summer's day can be difficult for a printer, as the ink will dry in quickly before you get it to the wash-off area. Speciality pigment binders and printable glues are particularly prone to clogging up screen meshes easily. So it may be a good idea to do these processes last of all to avoid having to chemically clean off the screen destroying your images also, and having to go through the whole re-exposure process again.

Useful tip: the chemical urea mixed in with your print paste will help reduce clogging in your screen mesh (30g urea to 100g print paste).

Always stack your screens away carefully, as screen mesh is easily torn if left against the edge of a table, or in a place where it can be easily knocked over.

Screen Frame

Screen frames are now mostly made of aluminium that is lightweight, easy to handle and less likely to rust like metal frames that are much heavier. Unless you have access to a screen-stretching machine, then you will need to get the screen restretched by your supplier. Some older frames are made of wood (that you can still buy, or even make yourself) and are useful on a small scale as you can restretch them by hand.

**Stacked screens of various sizes
at Central St Martins Art College.**

RESTRETCHING WOODEN FRAMES

1) Cut a piece of polyester filament large enough to cover an area the size of the front and sides of the frame. Stand the screen on its side and place one side of the mesh along the longer side edge of the screen frame, make the mesh as straight as possible. It is more secure if the mesh is doubled over when it is stapled to prevent any tears.

2) With a wall stapler, staple the mesh as straight as possible to the side of the frame at intervals of approximately 2.5cm all the way along one side.

3) Then go to the opposing side of the screen and pull the mesh as taut as you can from the middle, without distorting the weave of the mesh, and then staple this side in the same way. It is a good idea to get someone to help you either with the stapling or holding the mesh taut. A pair of stretching pliers will also help pull the mesh tighter.

4) Repeat on the other two opposing sides.

5) When you have finished, prod the middle of the screen mesh with your hand to check how taut the mesh is. If you can push it in by more than a centimetre, it may result in your images being too blurred when they are printed.

Pull the mesh as tight as possible to the other side of the screen frame.

When hand-stretching a screen, staple the screen mesh along one edge of the screen.

The wood may deteriorate and rot eventually, but you should still get a few years out of the frame.

Cleaning and Degreasing Screens

If you are reusing an old mesh with a photo stencil already exposed on it that needs removing, then you will have to give the screen a thorough chemical clean to remove the stencil and any ink that has dried into the screen mesh. For this you will need a high-powered hose or pressure washer – one used for cleaning cars or outside walls is fine. A deep sink is useful in an indoor environment, or somewhere out of the way out-side where the water can run off easily.

Remember to wear strong rubber gloves, a waterproof apron and goggles or face visor, as some of the cleaning chemicals contain products such as caustic soda and can easily be sprayed

Staple on the opposing side. Repeat on the other two sides of the frame.

back into your face. A high-pressure hose is also extremely noisy, so earplugs may be useful.

Companies use different product brands, so check with the manufacturer to see how their product should be used specifically, and if it is safe in a small workshop environment.

1) Firstly, you need to remove any packing tape or gum strip from the borders of the screen. Gum strip needs to be soaked in water and then peeled off. It is important to do this properly before you use the high-pressure hose, as you will find that the mashed-up gum strip will get caught up in the mesh of the screen causing blockages, and you will have to rewash.

2) Then remove the previous image or stencil, by spreading a stencil-removing chemical all over the screen evenly with a brush, and leave it to soak in for the recommended time. If you let it dry on the screen it can reverse the process.

3) Rinse the stencil remover off, then blast the screen with jets of water on both sides to remove the stencil. Keep checking the mesh in bright sunlight to see if it is properly cleaned off.

4) When the stencil has been successfully removed, if there are still blockages caused by dried ink, or ghost images still remaining on the screen, you will need to apply a screen wash for up to twenty-four hours, and then repeat the cleaning process.

5) Be extremely careful if there are small tears in the screen, as they will rip completely under the water pressure. Cover them up with strong tape.

6) If after repeated washes the screen won't clean then it may be at the end of its life span, and you will need to re-stretch. The more effort you put in to clean the screen after each image change, the more reusable it is, and the less likely to block up.

If your screen mesh is new, it will need degreasing with a degreasing gel, as any residue will resist the photo stencil emulsion causing the images to break down. Again, apply with a brush evenly over the screen for a few minutes, and blast off with water.

Getting a Positive Ready

For the process of making your image or motif into a photo stencil on screen, you will need to have an opaque positive of the image that can be drawn, painted or photocopied. The best positives are in black, as the image will need to be solid enough to resist ultraviolet light going through it; but any media that is non-transparent will do, such as white typing correction fluid, which is completely opaque.

Your drawing or painting materials for making your positive also need to work on a transparent or semi-transparent paper. Ordinary cartridge paper is too opaque to use and will come through onto the screen. A graphic design shop or your screen supplier will sell drafting film, which is a semi-clear film that can be painted or drawn on (each supplier has its own brand name). If you are on a budget, then tracing paper will do as a transparent background paper but is prone to cockling.

The best materials to use on film are process black, Indian ink, oil pastel (you could make direct rubbings from objects), acrylic if it is not applied too thickly, chinagraph pencil and even a soft pencil. For fine images Rotring ink pens are good, felt tips tend not to be opaque enough.

Experiment with your media, as you would on paper (*see* Chapter 1, mark-making). Check the opacity of the image by holding the drawn or painted image through a light source.

Black and white photocopies are usually fine to expose as the paper is quite thin, and you can also spread vegetable oil over the paper with a cloth to make it more transparent. You could draw or paint your design using any media just in black, onto regular paper, and then photocopy it onto thinner paper, to expose onto the screen.

Remember that producing your image in black or another opaque medium is only for the purpose of transferring it onto screen, and once on screen it can be printed in any colour.

Colour Separation

If you have produced a design using several colours, you will need to separate the colours out individually and expose them separately onto different screens. If every motif is put on one screen it will be virtually impossible to print the colours differently, unless there are spaces between the images, and the pattern will be exposed and printed as a whole solid area.

To do this manually, you should place your original design on a light source, and have a separate piece of semi-transparent paper or film for each colour of your design. Place the first sheet on top of the design and choose one colour, which you should then trace in black or opaque on the film or paper. Do the same for each colour, making sure you are accurate. So if your original design has four colours, then you should have four pieces of drawn or painted film representing each colour of your design.

A finished design that is to be silk-screen printed on a length of fabric, by Rhian Hancox.
Each colour will need to be separated into separate positives.

Tip forward and pull up firmly in one movement.

Pull back the emulsion at the top.

Your first few attempts may be messy, but this can be rectified.

If you run out of emulsion halfway up then refill the trough with emulsion quickly, and start the process again from the bottom, never from where the emulsion ran out.

If emulsion has spilled or has been applied unevenly or too thickly, then run the trough all the way up the screen without any ink in it, so it scrapes off all the excess. Hold the screen up and check that the emulsion has been distributed evenly. If there are thick patches, they will completely peel off after the screen has been exposed.

Once you have coated the screen, then it should be left in a horizontal position to dry. A shelf rack is useful to stack the screens. Never place newly coated screens on top of dry or half dry screens in case the coating material drips onto the one below, rendering them unusable, in which case you will have to go through the whole process again. Make sure they also dry in the dark, as any light will harden the emulsion, so you are unable to expose anything onto it. You may use a heater, indirectly, to speed up the drying process, which can take as little as half an hour. The screens can last up to two weeks in a dark environment with unexposed coating on before it begins to harden, depending on the type of emulsion you have bought.

Exposing your Screen

When the screen emulsion is dry, then your image will need to be exposed with ultraviolet light, and washed out in a large sink or washing-out booth with a gentle water jet. A professional screen exposure unit is recommended for this process but there are alternative methods of exposing your images on screen if you cannot access a unit.

1) When you are ready to expose the screen you will need to use clear tape to stick your image positives face down onto the coated screen mesh on the outside of the frame. Do not place the images too near the frame edge or it will be hard to print them, and if they are individual images for samples, try and leave some space between the images, so you can print them singly.

2) If you are using a professional exposure unit you will need to place the silk screen carefully on top of the glass top. Check that the surface is clean first, as any marks will also be exposed onto the screen. Make sure any loose screws or bars are removed from the screen or they may be sharp enough to penetrate through and tear the rubber lid, when it is vacuumed.

3) Double check you are happy with the positioning of the screen images – they may have accidentally been dislodged – and then fasten the lid of the exposure unit down over the top of the screen.

4) You will need to set the time for the exposure of your screen to ultraviolet light. Some machines do this in unit time and others in minutes and seconds, using a light meter.

SCREEN EXPOSURE EQUIPMENT

A professional unit will have a large, flat, glass surface containing an ultraviolet light source underneath. The unit will also have a vacuumed lid that closes down over the glass top, so the image is protected from outside light, and is exposed sharply.

If you buy your own unit it will need to be housed in its own room, to protect you from continual exposure to ultraviolet light. There are different types of machines on the market and different sizes, so obviously make sure it can accommodate your screen sizes comfortably, and it is compatible with the type of emulsion you are using. It is important to negotiate this with your supplier. They can advise you on exposure times, but you may need to do some tests yourself until you get the correct exposure time with your screen-coating emulsion.

Some suppliers may be able to help you find reconditioned machines to cut down on costs, or alternatively you may be able to go to an established workshop and use their equipment. If you need to transport a coated screen to a workshop for exposing, then carry it in a sealed bin liner to protect it from sunlight.

Alternative light sources for exposure can be obtained using photographic light bulbs, or a repro mercury vapour lamp, sold for this specific purpose. Your supplier can give you advice on exposure times and the distance of the screen from the light source for this. You will need a sheet of glass to fit over the top of the screen, to hold the image firmly in place or it will be exposed blurred. The screen will need to be placed on top of a blackout material. You may build your own unit by building a wooden box with a glass top containing a light source inside. You will need to have a blackout covering over the screen weighted down to prevent the images being exposed from being blurred.

A sunny day is also a useful light source, so the sunrays can expose the screen, but the results are very unpredictable.

All these methods will need experiments to determine exposure times, to accommodate your surroundings.

Place the positive face down on the outside of the dry coated screen.

BELOW: **Washing out an exposed screen. (Photograph by June Fish)**

Generally, photocopied images on paper will take longer because they are not completely translucent. Drawn or painted images on tracing paper and drafting film will require less time, and completely opaque pieces such as black paper will have the shortest exposure time.

The machine will have a switch to turn on the vacuum and this will tightly suction the screen down, to prevent the images blurring.

5) When the screen is tightly covered so you can see the shape of it underneath the rubber, then turn on the ultraviolet light switch.

Ultraviolet light is extremely harmful to your eyes, so leave the room while the screen is being exposed. Your machine should count down the time and automatically turn off the ultraviolet light source.

6) When the exposure has finished, release the vacuumed lid and wait for it to de-suction, and then remove the screen, but don't take the paper images off the mesh until you are ready to wash-out the screen.

The screen coating will have undergone a photochemical reaction, changing colour slightly, having become hardened and made semi-permanent under the ultraviolet light. The emulsion where the opaque images have blocked out the light will have remained unexposed and the same colour as before, so the emulsion in these areas hasn't hardened.

7) Now take the screen to a large sink and wash out on both sides preferably using a water hose. After a minute or so, the underexposed sections will begin to fall out leaving your images as clear shapes on the screen mesh. Do not overwash the screen or too much of the emulsion will fall out. If you find that your image is not appearing very well, then you could lightly use a sponge or brush to help it on its way.

The image does not come out easily if the screen has been over-exposed to ultraviolet light, if you have left it in normal light or if the screen has been left for too long coated with emulsion in a dark room.

If the opposite happens, and all the emulsion comes off, then your screen has been underexposed to light, or the paper you used was too thick.

8) While the screen is drying off after washing, it is a good time to apply gum strip or packing tape around all four sides of the screen, on the inside and on the outside. This should be placed in strips halfway over the frame and the mesh, to cover the gap where the emulsion did not reach the edge, or ink will come through here when you are printing.

9) Once the screen is dry, you need to check for pinholes caused by small bubbles when you coated the screen or by dust particles. These need to be covered with thin brush strokes of either the coating emulsion, a special stop out or even typing correction fluid. Apply the cover on the outside part of the mesh. If you use coating emulsion you will have to re-expose the screen with ultraviolet light to make it permanent. The screen does not need washing out again though.

Preparation for Printing

If you are exposing and printing the screen in the same workshop, it is a good idea to utilize your time, and begin preparing your printing surface while you are waiting for your screens to be ready. Much time is spent waiting for silk screens to dry during the exposing and printing processes, so organize your time, and prepare any other materials.

Make sure the printing surface you are using is clean from its previous usage. Unclean and bumpy surfaces, contaminated materials and a lack of considered preparation cause most errors in printing and dyeing. This may leave frustrating permanent ink stains or poor quality prints on your fabric, that spoil your design.

Useful materials, which will aid your preparation are:

- Clean backing cloth for your print table (heavyweight cotton)
- Iron
- Pins

An exposed screen being taped on the inside and outside of the frame, to prevent ink seeping through when printing.

- Pencil and metre ruler
- Ream of newsprint
- Gum strip and masking tape
- Bowl of water, sponges, cloths and hand brush.
- Squeegee
- Print table.

You may be fortunate enough to have access to a professional standard print table that is at least 3m long, and wide enough to accommodate a dress-sized screen. This type of print table may also have a registration bar for repeat printing on a length of fabric. If long runs of printed fabric are important for your work or business, then you may need to consider a large studio space and the purchase of a professionally made print table. If this is out of the question financially then source out a print workshop in your area that hires out space and equipment, or an art college with a textile course where they may be willing to hire out space in holiday periods.

Most print tables have a waterproof top layer that is made from vinyl, rubber or neoprene. Make sure prior to use that this is washed down with a nylon brush and water. If you allow ink stains to build up on the surface, it will eventually become uneven to print on, so keep on top of it.

1) When it is washed and dried, the table surface should be coated with a gum, to allow fabric to be ironed onto it. To do this you can use gum arabic or Manutex (recipes on how to mix these are in the section under thickeners). Dissolve the gum in water until it is slightly runnier than a printing consistency and pour a small portion onto the table. Using a squeegee, spread the gum evenly around the print table, leaving no gaps or pools of gum. Any excess gum can be scooped off the edge of the table back into the bucket and reused.
2) Wait for the gum to dry and then place a clean backing cloth on top, covering the length and width of the table, making sure there are no creases.
3) With a hot iron, starting from the middle of the table, iron the fabric to the gum. The table gum melts with the heat allowing it to stick the cloth to the table. Push the iron out in each direction from the middle of the table to iron out any potential creases to the edges.
4) If your print table is large, than a second person is useful to help direct the cloth and keep it taut while you're ironing.

If you have a heavyweight furnishing fabric you can dispense with the backing cloth and iron your printing fabric directly to the gummed table. Backing cloths help protect your print table, particularly if you are using glues, or heavy staining inks such as discharge.

MAKING YOUR OWN PRINT TABLE

If your requirements are smaller, and you are producing one-off sample-size prints, then it is possible to customize your own print table.

1) Firstly, find a sturdy table with enough length and width for your screen sizes. If it is not weighty enough you may have to attach it to the floor to stop it moving when you are printing.

2) You will need to create a padded print surface – felt blankets are ideal for this. Stretch the blanket over the table and staple it to the sides of the table. At least two layers will be needed.

3) Then cover the top with vinyl or rubber, and staple it over the blankets, again around the sides of the table. This will be easy to replace if it becomes too ink-stained.

Setting Up a Screen and Table for Repeat Printing

1) Once you have put your design into repeat (*see* Chapter 2) and separated the colours if necessary, the images then need to be accurately positioned on screen for exposing. You will need a dress or furnishing size screen that will cover the width of your fabric allowing you to repeat the fabric length continuously. Make sure your positives are measured, using your crosses (*see* Chapter 2) to line them up straight, from the end of the screen that has the bolts and fittings, before exposing the screen. If you are printing more than one colour try to use the same size screens, and place all your positives at exactly the same distances from the frame edges on all four sides, this will save time later.
2) The screen should be fitted with two bolts (or screws for wood), one at either end of the top of the screen to allow adjustments, and an L- or T-shaped bar between them to rest against your repeat stops. You will need an adjustable spanner and screwdriver.
3) Keep your image positives in a good condition, as you will need them to line up your screen and repeat distance on the print table.

ABOVE: **A length of fabric on the print table, in the middle of being repeat printed. (Photograph by June Fish)**

RIGHT: **(i) When setting up a screen for repeat printing, use the design to help it line up with the registration bar. Make sure the design is as straight as possible. The measurements from both As, both Bs and both Cs should be the same distance.**

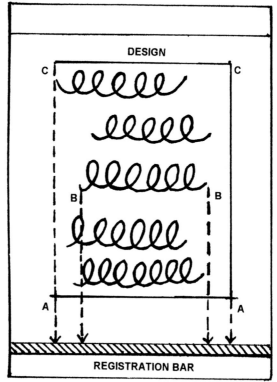

4) When the screen is dry and taped up ready for printing, lay it on the table almost against the registration bar (but leave some room for manoeuvre) to get a general idea where the screen image begins. Remove the screen and place the corresponding positive in this area. Using your crosses and prominent points where the image joins up for repeat on either side of the positive, measure the distance from the bar (i).

5) Check that all the distances are the same to the bar. When you are satisfied, attach the positive to the table. Lay the first screen on top and line it up accurately with its corresponding

ii

iii

iv

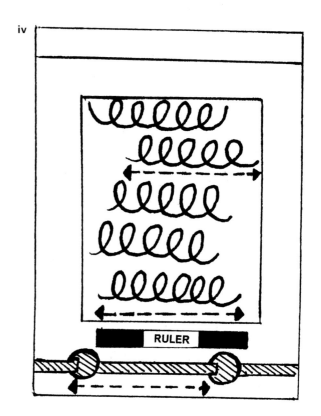

RULER

ABOVE: **(ii) Place the screen on top of the design, and adjust the bolts so they are firm against the bar.**

ABOVE RIGHT: **(iii) Fit a L- or T-shaped bar, resting firmly against the first stop.**

RIGHT: **(iv) Measure the repeat distance.**

positive underneath. Then adjust your bolts so they rest against the registration bar (ii).

6) Attach your L- or T-shaped bar to the screen, and rest the first registration stop firmly against the L- or T-bar (iii).

7) Lay your second positive on top of the first in the correct place, and then put the second screen on top, and repeat the process. Do this for all your screens.

8) Once you have your first repeat stop in place, measure your repeat distance, from left to right on your positive, at points where the repeat joins. Then set your stops at this distance, making sure they are firmly attached to the bar (iv).

v

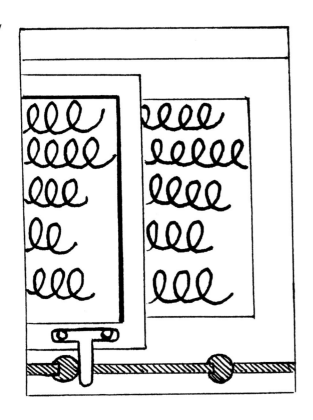

Fit the stops at the repeat distance, and try out the print onto paper, to check the repeat distance is correct.

vi

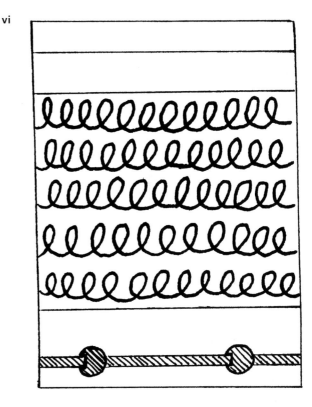

The repeat should flow with no awkward joins.

9) To check that the repeat distance is correct, print the image where you set your first stop, and then one print on either side, to see if the repeat matches up (v and vi).

10) If the screens are different sizes, or the images have been exposed in different places, you will need to reset the registration stops after each colour is printed.

11) When you are printing a length of fabric, ensure that the screen bolts are always firmly against the registration bar and that the L- or T-shaped bar is always placed against one side of the registration stop, all left side or all right side. Always print at every other registration stop, allowing the print to dry before printing the ones in between to avoid ink being picked up on the back of the screen and being reprinted elsewhere.

12) Two people should be involved with printing, on either side of the table.

Pinning

Once you have ironed-on your backing cloth, you will need to pin your fabric down on top. Pinning is particularly important for lightweight and stretchy fabrics, to keep them as straight and taut as possible, so that the image does not distort when printed.

For repeat lengths in particular, it is important to pin the fabric in a straight line. Using a pencil and ruler draw a straight line parallel with your table edge, and registration bar, and a few inches in, to allow the frame of the screen to fit in comfortably, and correspond with where your image starts to be printed.

Lay your fabric out with one length edge against the length of the line, and start pinning from this edge, starting in the middle and working your way to either end. The pins should be spaced about 2.5cm (1in) apart, facing into the fabric. Do not pin into the print table, but just into the backing cloth below or you will puncture the table surface.

Once you have done one side, then do exactly the same on the opposite side of the length. Draw another straight line where the fabric reaches to, keeping the fabric taut as you pin. Then pin the end widths of the fabric.

Printing and Using a Squeegee

When you are ready to print, place the screen on top of your fabric in the correct place. Spoon a layer of printing ink an inch wide inside the screen, along the length of the image you wish to print, but not on it. If you do not put enough ink on, it will run out halfway through, and you will need to quickly overprint with more ink from the beginning. Remember to block out

A student pinning fabric onto a clean backing cloth.
(Photograph by June Fish)

Squeegees of various sizes.

anything you are not printing with paper or tape on the outside of the screen. Never put ink directly on the image you are printing unless you want a multi-coloured effect all over.

It is important to have a good quality squeegee to print with. Most squeegees have a wooden or aluminium handle, with a rubber blade, for dragging the ink across and through the silk-screen mesh. A slightly rounded rubber blade is better for fabric printing, and a squarer blade is better for paper printing.

The squeegee should be held at an angle of about 45 degrees from the screen, behind the ink, and should be pulled cleanly across the screen mesh. If you hold the squeegee upright you will find it hard to apply enough pressure to push the ink through the mesh. If it is too horizontal then the ink is more likely to ride up the blade of the squeegee. If you stop halfway through your printing, it will leave a thick line of ink that will come through onto the fabric. Another pull will even out the ink to rectify this.

When printing, place the ink along the top edge of the screen.

Pull the squeegee at a 45 degree angle, in one firm pull across the screen.

Make sure your squeegee is always slightly wider than the image you are printing, otherwise you will leave streaky lines on the areas of printed fabric where you have had to overlap the printing because your squeegee was not wide enough. At the other end of the scale, try not to use a huge squeegee for a small area, as you may end up accidentally printing other images on your screen, and you may not apply even pressure on the area you wish to print.

It is useful to have a range of different-size squeegees for small sample areas, and one large one that fits a dress or furnishing size screen if you intend to produce a length of fabric. When you are working on a large scale it is probably a good idea to have a second person to hold the screen for you, if you do not have a table rail to rest the screen against. A heavy weight on the screen will also stop it from moving. Keep the squeegee clean; if ink is continually left to dry on in layers, then it will lose its sharp edge and create streaky prints. The rubber blade will eventually deteriorate under the effects of strong chemicals (polyurethane keeps longer), and will need to be replaced. It is possible to buy the rubber on its own and slot it in to the handle yourself to save costs. Wooden-handled squeegees will need protective varnish, to make them more waterproof. The amount of pulls of ink with your squeegee depends on the thickness of your paper or fabric. Paper normally needs one pull, lightweight fabrics one or two pulls, and heavier fabrics may need at least four to six pulls. This also depends on the type of ink, so sampling is recommended first.

When you are finished, scrape the excess ink off your screen, and remove it in one clean movement from your fabric and wash-out the ink immediately with a gentle water jet.

Good Workshop Practice

Carelessness and lack of preparation cause most printing errors. It is important to be tidy and methodical in your approach to avoid making unnecessary printing mistakes that will more than likely become permanent on your fabric.

Always keep your printing inks under the table, as they can get easily knocked over.

Regularly change your backing cloth, as inks will eventually seep through onto your new fabric. Keep the print table clean, and do not use it for cutting on.

For large screen prints two people will be necessary.

136

Have a supply of newsprint or newspaper handy to cover up areas of your fabric or backing cloth that you do not want to print on. Plan out where your prints are going in advance. Avoid placing the screen back down on an area that has just been printed where the ink is still wet, as the wet ink will get picked up on the outside of the screen, and it will reprint when the screen is placed back down again.

If the screen and squeegee are getting covered in excessive ink along with your hands, then wash it off and start again, as you will risk drops of ink being dropped on your fabric.

Always scoop up excess ink off your screen and squeegee immediately after you have finished printing, to prevent ink being dropped on the floor and to prevent polluting the water system more than necessary. Always use water-based materials.

When washing your screen out, make sure you wash the inside of the frame properly, or ink will collect in the edges of the mesh and frame and will be picked up on your next print.

Do not leave ink on the screen for too long before washing off, particularly on warm days as it will dry in very quickly, and you will end up chemically cleaning the whole screen off, including your images and having to start all over again. If there are some blockages from printing you could try using a high-pressure water gun very carefully with the water fanned out as much as possible, and blast out the ink. You do risk destroying your image though.

Tidy up at the end of each day.

Print Recipes

Listed on the next few pages are a range of standard recipes for mixing and using textile printing inks. If you are buying materials from one particular manufacturer, they may supply slightly different brands and products and so you should ask them for a specific recipe sheet as it may differ slightly in its preparation and fixation.

Remember that this is also a basic guideline, and there is plenty of room for experimentation (*see* Chapter 3). Once you have experience and a good understanding about what the dyes and chemicals do, then you may wish to alter the quantities and change the process to discover your own effects and colour palette. Many of the recipes combine well together, such as reactive and devoré, so try combinations of overprinting or mixing dye colours into other recipe effects. This should obviously take into account health and safety. It is important not to put yourself at any risks.

Equipment for Mixing Printing Inks

Before starting, make sure you equip your workshop with the following materials:

- Strong plastic pots, with tight-fitting lids, 1l in size or less. Regular sizes will enable you to keep track of quantities (some plastic cups are fine for use over a day or two but will eventually dissolve and an airtight lid stops the paste going off as quickly)
- Wood or plastic stirrers
- Plastic shovels for decanting thickener powders
- Measuring jug
- Measuring tube for liquid chemicals
- Scales, for small measurements (electronic scales are ideal)
- Metal jugs for dissolving some dye powders
- Metal spoons
- Electric whisk
- Stove. A portable stove is preferable to using a kitchen cooker, where powders are liable to end up on kitchen work surfaces
- Gloves, dust masks and apron.

Keep all your recipe sheets in plastic sleeves, and keep an accurate record of samples of everything you do.

Quantities, Shelf Life and Consistency of Printing Ink

Only mix up enough ink for the prints you are doing at that particular time, unless you know you will be using more before it expires. This will ease your worries about safe disposal. Below are some guidelines to the quantities you should mix up:

- If you are at the early stages of sampling on small-scale pieces of fabric – *100–150g of print paste is sufficient.*
- Scarves and one-off garment pieces – *200–300g of print paste.*
- 3m + length of fabric – *500–1,000g of print paste* (this depends on the weight of the fabric: heavier fabrics will need a larger number of pulls of ink. A sheer silk may only need one pull of ink through the silk screen whereas a heavyweight wool or devoré velvet will sometimes need up to eight or ten layers of ink. You need to work this out at the sampling stage).

When purchasing your chemicals, inks and dyes in bulk, make sure you have good storage facilities, as contamination, water-logging or drying out of products can easily occur. Pigment inks should, for example, have a shelf life of up to six months, but can dry up completely overnight if kept in a warm studio in an open pot. If possible, it is useful to keep your inks in a cool environment such as a fridge.

The fresher the inks are the better the results, but many do have a good shelf life if kept in the right conditions. This is certainly aided by investing in a variety of different sized pots with tightly fitting lids. Omitting certain chemicals that are in the recipes and only adding them when you are about to use the ink can also prolong its usage. Some of the thickeners are organic so can quickly go mouldy or runny in warm conditions, also an ammonia-type odour can indicate that the printing ink is no longer in a good enough condition to use. A guide to the ink shelf life is as follows:

Pigment – up to six months

Reactive – up to a month (longer without sodium bicarbonate added)

Acid – up to a month (longer without ammonium oxalate added)

White and Colour Discharge – up to 2 days (much longer without decrolin or formosol added)

Devoré, Cellulosic – several months

Devoré, Protein – 1 day

Water-Based Adhesive – several months

Printing Thickeners

The function of a thickening agent is to aid the transfer of dye colour onto the fabric, mainly through printed methods. Pigment ink is the only print paste that comes already made up into a binder with the correct consistency. The thickening pastes or binders for the other inks come in powder form and need to be dissolved in water to form a gum in the correct consistency to screen-print with. The print paste should be a similar consistency to syrup, and if picked up on a spoon should fall back into the pot in a regular slow movement. If it is too runny, the print will bleed when printed; if it is too thick, it will clog up the screen and not print properly.

When deciding what thickening agents to use, its most important qualities will be its compatibility with the dyes and auxiliary chemicals, and its ability not to break down during steaming or fixing, as it holds in the dye that may bleed all over the fabric.

Pigment binder is the only binder to remain in the fabric permanently once printed. This affects the feel of the fabric if used in large areas. All the other thickeners must be completely removed by washing after the fabric has been steamed, as they are mainly organic in nature and will deteriorate. This just leaves the printed dye in the fabric so restores it to a natural feel. This is particularly beneficial for sheer and delicate fabrics, where removal thickening agents are preferable to pigment binder.

There is a variety of printing gums; the most useful ones include the following.

INDULCA (locust bean gum)

Indulca is the most commonly used brand name for locust bean gum and it is probably the most versatile thickener to have available at your disposal. It is extracted from seeds of the carob tree, and is purchased for printing use in a 'sand'-like consistency. It should be added to and dissolved in water (100g of indulca to 1l of water). A high-speed mixer will speed up the process, and it can be ready to use within an hour. Only mix up enough (kept in a sealed container) to last between two to four weeks depending on conditions. If you cannot store it in a cool place during the summer months once made up, the gum tends to go runny very quickly. In powder form indulca should last indefinitely.

Because of its stability in alkaline and acidic conditions, indulca works well with acid, disperse, discharge and devoré paste.

MANUTEX (seaweed, sodium alginate)

Manutex is a common brand name for a seaweed-based thickener that began to be widely used in the 1950s, with the invention of reactive dyes for cellulose fibres with which it works best. It is split into two types, Manutex F and Manutex RS. Both types need to be dissolved and mixed in water. The powder gradually expands once in water, so it needs to sit for at least one hour.

Manutex F works better if you need to overprint colours, or are printing fine lines, because of its low viscosity and high solid content (mix 100g of Manutex F powder with 1l of water). It can be used with reactives, directs and disperse. Manutex F can also be used to make table gum, to help stick down backing cloths.

Manutex RS works slightly better with reactive dye; it has a lower solid content and is used mainly on thicker fabrics or single prints (mix 45g of Manutex RS powder with 1l of water). It can be used with reactives and direct dyes.

The above thickeners will probably be the main ones you will need to use, but some of the others listed below may be worth considering.

GUM ARABIC

This gum was traditionally used for printing silk with a high definition, but is expensive and goes off very easily, giving off a very pungent odour. It needs to be heated to boiling point in water to dissolve (400g of gum arabic to 1l of water). It is very useful as a table gum in a more runny state.

GUAR GUM

Guar gum is quite versatile and similar to Indulca. It works well in acidic conditions, and can be used for acid, disperse, discharge and devoré printing (mix 120g guar gum into 1l of water).

CRYSTAL GUM

The common brand name for this is Nafka. This is particularly good for acid and disperse printing, and was commonly used on silk because of its high definition. (Mix with a whisk, 200g of Nafka to 1l of water. Leave to stand overnight, or heat the mixture up to dissolve it.)

STARCH ETHERS

Solvitose C5 is the most common brand name for starch ether thickener, which is suitable in alkaline conditions and can be used in most print pastes except for acids. It is particularly useful for protein devoré printing (the recipe can be found in the devoré section).

Pigment

Pigment ink is the most widely used of all the inks, because it works on all fabrics and needs very little in the way of finishing. As well as producing a standard ink, pigment now also has a variety of special binders that create different effects, such as opacity, gloss, metallic and heat-sensitive effects (see Chapter 4). The colour range is large and also includes fluorescents.

Its drawbacks are its finish, which stiffens the fabric, making it unsuitable on lightweight fabrics, and if used in large areas can also affect the drape of fabric. This problem is accentuated with the specialist binders that are thicker than the standard colour.

STANDARD COLOUR

The standard colour ink works on fabric that is white or lighter than the colour of the ink. It will disappear into darker colour fabrics. The ink is comprised of a standard pigment binder (white in appearance, translucent when dry) mixed with a concentrated pigment colour.

Using a strong plastic pot, fill it with enough binder to print the size of your image, then drop in a small quantity of concentrated colour and stir in well or it will be streaky when printed.

You will need approximately 1g to 6g of colour pigment for every 100g of pigment binder.

The quantity is reduced for paler colours, and concentrated colours can also be intermixed with each other.

Once printed leave the fabric to dry, and then fix the ink by baking or curing. The printed pigment needs to be fixed at a temperature of 150° for 5min. You can do this with an iron or heat transfer press, but make sure to be careful so that you don't scorch the fabric.

Polyester fabrics have less surface adhesion, so can spread slightly, and need extra care when drying and baking.

Pigment is fully washable when fixed, and can be used to print on paper although it can be slightly 'bubbly' in appearance.

Reactives

Reactives (the brand name is usually Procion) supply an excellent broad range of printing ink colours, offering good wash fastness, and leaving the fabric with the same handle as before printing. Both the P/SP and MX range are suitable for printing with, although the P/SP range is more stable and has a longer shelf life once the inks are mixed up. The MX range can also be used for dyeing though, making them more economical.

The disadvantage of using reactives is with the finishing processes. The ink needs to be steamed and washed extremely carefully to remove any lingering traces of the printing gum and excess dye; some colours are prone to bleeding, so may have to be continually re-washed to achieve a satisfactory result.

REACTIVE (PROCION) P/SP

Print quantity 100g (sample amount)

Full shade of colour:

- 4g dye

- 10g urea

- 4g resist salt L

- 5g sodium bicarbonate

- enough warm water to dissolve the dye

- 100g Manutex F gum

1) Weigh out, and dissolve the dye and urea in warm water. Reduce the quantity of dye for paler shades, and never exceed the full quantity if you wish to mix several colours together.

2) Add the resist salt L, and the sodium bicarbonate (already dissolved in warm water) into the mixture. (Sodium bicarbonate will also work when used on cotton.)

3) Stir in the Manutex F gum (already dissolved). Leave the paste to sit for a few minutes to allow everything to dissolve properly.

4) Print your fabric only after you have tested your colours and amount of pulls necessary with the screen and squeegee. Wash your screen carefully after printing.

5) Once the fabric is dry, it will need to be steamed for 20min, or baked for 5min at a temperature of 150°C (*refer* to the section on finishing). Steaming does not need to be carried out immediately.

6) After fixation wash the fabric in cool water until it runs clear of dye colour, and the Manutex has been removed. It helps to lay the fabric as flat as possible (a bath is useful), to prevent the migration of unfixed ink from one area to another.

7) Then wash in hot water with a drop of Metapex, until the water runs clear and the fabric has stopped bleeding. You may have to repeat this process several times; do not allow the fabric to dry out until you are satisfied.

REACTIVE (PROCION) MX

Prior to mixing the print recipe, the fabric should be soaked in sodium carbonate (soda ash). The fabric can either be dipped in a bath of water with sodium carbonate, for several minutes, or sprayed with the solution. You will need:

- 30g of soda ash for every litre of water

Leave the fabric to drip dry. Then mix the print recipe exactly the same as the recipe for Procion P/SP, except that you omit the sodium bicarbonate or sodium carbonate. The paste should then last for several weeks.

As well as steaming and baking, the fabric can also be fixed by air-hanging overnight, and then ironed for several minutes at 120°C, which is useful if you do not have access to a steamer.

Wash-out your fabric in the same way as for the Procion P/SP recipe.

Hand-Painting Dyes onto Screen and Fabrics

MX dyes are ideal for hand-painting directly onto fabric or silk screen (*see* Chapter 3).

Prepare the fabric with soda ash as previously stated, and mix your dye for painting with, omitting all or most of the Manutex and replacing it with water. Keep to the same proportions as in the recipe above, but you will probably need much less dye powder and auxiliary chemicals for printing.

If you are painting onto silk screen, you will still need Manutex to print the painted images through onto your fabric once they are dry.

The fabric will then need fixing and washing in the same way as printed reactives.

Acid Printing

Acid printing inks are provided with colour by acid dyes used for dyeing protein fibres, and provide a broad, vibrant colour range, generally colourfast and with a reasonably long shelf life. The main disadvantage is a long steaming time, one hour, and the colours can intensify during the steaming process, so can look darker than when printing. As well as protein fibres, acid can be printed onto nylon.

Discharge Printing

The aim of discharge printing is to enable lighter colour prints to be printed onto darker colour backgrounds. This is achieved by adding a 'reducing agent' to the print paste, which acts like bleach and completely removes the background colour, allowing the new print paste colour to replace it.

The advantage of discharge paste is that it produces a variety of colourfast, vibrant colours particularly on silk, and leaves the fabric with the same handle and texture as before, so is ideal for delicate fabrics. The only other alternative for printing lighter colours onto darker backgrounds is to use an opaque pigment binder (*see* Chapter 4) that prints and sits permanently over the top of the background colour, leaving the fabric quite stiff and flattening any texture.

The disadvantage of discharge colours is mainly concerned with health and safety. The reducing agents are called Decrolin and Formosol, and need to be used carefully as they carry a 'harmful' label. These chemicals should only be used in a well-ventilated area. A proper fume mask is preferable, as the drying and steaming process can exacerbate the fumes, leading to nausea and headaches. I do not recommend using these chemicals at home.

You also need to make sure that you are printing onto dischargeable dyed grounds (*see* Chapter 6). Many pre-dyed fabrics may not work at all, so you may have to do all the dyeing yourself to be sure. Some fabrics that only partially discharge may yield interesting textures and colours.

Remember, if you are discharge printing over already dyed and printed fabrics, these must be fixed properly before reprinting, as they will need to be rewashed after discharge printing.

Keep the inks in a sealed pot at all times, until disposal. Once the reducing chemical is added the life span of the ink is only approximately two days (*see* box p.142).

ACID

Print quantity – 100g (sample amount)

Full shade of colour:

▨ 4g dye

▨ 4ml Perminal KB

▨ 5g of urea

▨ 5g of ammonium oxalate

▨ enough warm water to dissolve dye and oxalate

▨ 100g Indulca

1) Dissolve the dye and urea in a small quantity of warm water (reduce the quantities for paler shades), followed by the Perminal KB.

2) Dissolve the ammonium oxalate in hot water, and add with the Indulca gum to the rest of the mixture.

3) Print and dry the fabric, and steam for at least 45min, nylon is less at 30min. Steaming does not need to be carried out immediately.

4) Wash out the fabric in cool water, lay the sample as flat as possible in a sink, and wash until the water runs clear of dye colour, and the Indulca has been removed. Follow with a hot-water wash, and a drop of neutral detergent, until the water runs clear.

Acid dyes can also be hand-painted directly onto the silk screen, or directly onto the fabric by omitting the Indulca completely, or using it to print through the acid dye on the silk screen when it has dried (*see* Chapter 3). The fabric still needs to be steamed or air-hung overnight.

WHITE DISCHARGE PASTE

White discharge paste is the easiest to mix up, and useful if you are testing out dyed background colours for their ability to discharge.

Print quantity – 100g (sample amount)

- 5 to 20g of Formosol (cotton, silk) or Decrolin (wool, synthetics)

- Enough cold water to dissolve chemical

- 5ml glyezin BC

- 100g Indulca

1) Put enough cold water in a plastic pot to dissolve either the Formosol or Decrolin.

2) Add the chemical in a well-ventilated area (with a dust mask on). The quantity you add depends on the effect you want. Add the full amount if you want the fabric to go to white, less if you want to just lighten the base colour.

3) Then add the glyezin BC and stir, to dissolve the powder.

4) Pour in the Indulca, making sure it is mixed in well. Leave to dissolve for a few minutes, before printing.

5) The printed discharge paste appears transparent on the fabric, and only appears after steaming, so you will need to be extremely careful when printing, as you will not be able to see the results until the fabric is off the print table.

6) Once the fabric is printed, and dried naturally, it should then be steamed for 10min. The fabric should be steamed immediately after drying, or kept sealed in a bag overnight for steaming the next day.

7) Baking or ironing for 1min also works, but gives off intense fumes.

8) After steaming, wash the fabric in cold water, washing out the Indulca gum.

9) Then wash the fabric in detergent to remove any traces of the chemical aroma.

10) Spin or dry the fabric naturally.

You may find in warm, sunny conditions the discharge print may partly discharge itself out while on the print table. It is still worth steaming the fabric to make sure it is fully discharged. If the white discharge print has spread, reduce the amount of Formosol and Decrolin.

Illuminating Discharge Colours

Illuminating colours or dyes can be added into a white or clear discharge paste, to create a colour discharge. Illuminating colours are non-dischargeable dyes, which means they are not affected or bleached out by the discharge chemical. The best dyes to use for this are a small range of basic dyes (ask your supplier which one they recommend**)**. A selection of non-dischargeable acid and reactive dyes also work well, and are produced specifically for this purpose.

The results on silk are best, as the colours are extremely vibrant, wool also works well, but on cotton the results tend to be very washed out and pale (pigment discharge yields better results on cotton).

Some of these dyes have a medium or high hazard label, and can stain your skin for days if you do not wear gloves. Make sure the dyes are used following the guidelines on your health and safety data sheet (*see* p. 149).

Experiment with mixing multiple colours together at the print paste mixing stage, to develop your colour range, and by partially overprinting individual colours on top of each other to produce a third colour. Discharge colours can also be overprinted onto reactive and acid prints to create more variations, as some of these colours are very dischargeable. This can all be done at the same time on the print table and steamed together, using the steam times for acid and reactive. Keep an accurate record of results for future reference.

ILLUMINATING DISCHARGE

Print quantity – 100g (sample amount)

▨ 0.5g to 4g of illuminating dye colour

▨ 20g Formosol for silk or cotton, or 20g Decrolin for wool

▨ 4ml glyezin BC

▨ enough cold water to dissolve the chemical

▨ 100g Indulca

The quantity of dye reflects the depth of colour you wish to obtain.

1) Mix the dye with glyezin and water, to dissolve the dye powder.

2) Add the Formosol or Decrolin and stir in well.

3) Add the Indulca, and follow the same process as for white discharge, for steaming and washing. When washing out your fabric try to lay it as flat as possible in a sink, to avoid the migration of unfixed colour.

4) If there are white haloes appearing around your colour discharge print, then reduce the amount of Formosol and Decrolin you are using.

PIGMENT DISCHARGE

Print quantity – 100g (sample amount)

▨ 6g pigment colour

▨ 100g discharge binder or 50g pigment binder/50g Indulca

▨ 5g to 20g dissolved Formosol/Decrolin

1) Dissolve the Formosal or Decrolin with a small quantity of water. The amount of reducing agent depends on how strong you want the effect to stand out.

2) Then add the binder. Slowly add drops of concentrated pigment colour, until you are satisfied with the shade.

3) Once you have printed and dried the fabric you will still need to steam for 10min and wash the fabric in warm water and detergent.

4) If white haloes appear around the discharge print, reduce the amount of Formosol or Decrolin.

Pigment Discharge

The pigment ink range can be used for discharging onto cellulose fibres such as cotton. You will need to use an alternative to the standard pigment binder though, as it does not mix well with the discharge chemicals. Formosol and Decrolin tend to make the binder too runny to print with. Your supplier may make a special discharge pigment binder for this purpose – one brand is called Magna Discharge Base AB. The main drawback with this type of pigment discharge is that the binder will remain permanently in the fabric, changing the handle slightly by making it stiffer.

An alternative way of creating a discharge binder is to mix half the standard pigment binder with half Indulca, enabling the Indulca to be washed out afterwards.

The binder can be mixed with standard pigment colours to create colour discharges, with varying degrees of success as not all of the colours will work with discharge. Your supplier will be able to indicate which colours are the most suitable. They are generally categorized from A to E for dischargeability, similarly to dyes (*see box, above*).

Devoré Paste

Devoré printing is a controlled method of burning out one type of fibre from a fabric made up of mixed fibres, creating sheer, almost translucent areas of pattern in the finished fabric. The chemicals used for burning out the fibres can be mixed into a screen-printable paste that won't affect the screen mesh.

The paste can also be painted onto the fabric by hand, for a bolder outcome. The printed fabrics then need to undergo a heat process for the burn-out to take place.

There are three main types of devoré, that all burn out one particular type of fibre. The most commonly used is *cellulose devoré* for burning out viscose, linen and cotton, *protein devoré* for burning out animal fibres such as wool and mohair, and *lurex devoré* that burns-out metallic fibres from fabrics such as lamé.

To ensure that the fabric is left without any holes, after the devoré process, it is important that you obtain the correct fibre blends in the fabric. If you intend to burn out the cotton content of the fabric, then the other portion of fabric should be made of silk or polyester and so on, which is unaffected by cellulose devoré paste. The different fibres in the fabric should also be woven or knitted with both types of fibre in the warp and the weft, to ensure that no holes are created. Many fabric companies and textile suppliers normally sell a range of fabric mixes suitably constructed for the devoré process. The most common mixes are silk/viscose velvet, where the viscose pile is burnt away, and cotton/polyester leaving a sheer polyester weave behind after printing and burning.

Deviations are possible though, as you might want to create a different type of effect, such as burning controlled holes straight through a fabric that is made from one type of fibre. This works with densely constructed fabrics such as wool felt, as the holes are contained, and the fabric stays in shape. For a more shredded effect, experiment with mixed-fibre fabrics that are not constructed specifically for the devoré process. It is possible to skim the surface off piled fabrics, particularly cotton corduroy or velvet, so the effect is a small indentation and embossed effect, instead of completely removing the whole pile. This requires some testing and precision to avoid burning holes in the fabric, but can give interesting results.

All devoré fabrics can be printed on before or after going through the devoré process. They can also be cross dyed (*see* Chapter 6), so plan out any other processes ahead to maximize the visual look of your patterned fabric.

Before making use of any of the devoré recipes, ensure that you have a strong pair of gloves, dust mask and eye wear, to protect against the chemicals. Only loosen cellulose fibres in water, and experiment with baking and steaming times before you start, as the whole cloth can be completely burnt or may disintegrate.

A cellulose devoré print onto silk viscose fabrics, by Amanda French.

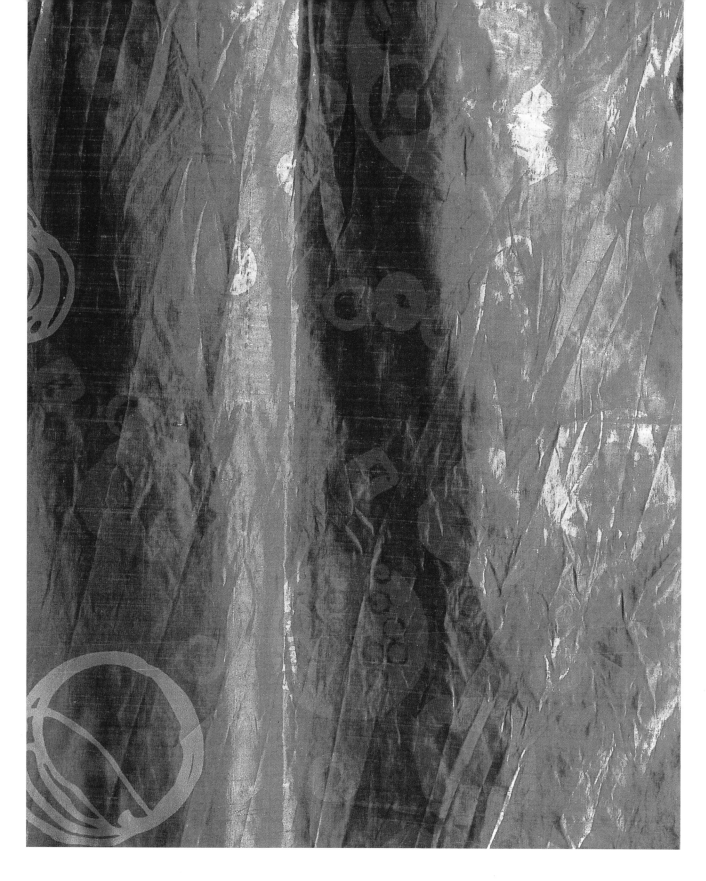

A lurex devoré print, burning out metallic fibres, by Amanda French.

CELLULOSE DEVORÉ

Common fabric mixes are: viscose/silk, cotton/polyester, cotton and linen/polyester.

For a sample amount of 100g:

- 30g aluminium sulphate
- 5ml glycerine
- 100g Indulca
- Small quantity of water to dissolve aluminium sulphate

1) Dissolve the aluminium sulphate with the water and glycerine, in a well-ventilated area, wearing dust mask and gloves.

2) Add the Indulca and stir in the mixture carefully. You may find the paste works better after several days, and lasts for several weeks.

3) Print your fabric, making sure you pull enough paste through to penetrate the fabric, unless you want a more subtle effect. Viscose/silk satin needs up to six pulls with the squeegee, and velvet may require ten pulls.

4) Velvet should also be printed on the back of the pile for the best results, so you may need to have your imagery back to front on screen, particularly if you are using writing, in order for it to appear the right way up on the pile side of the fabric.

5) Once you have printed, allow the fabric to dry, and then bake the fabric, for either 10min in a baking cabinet at 150°C, or in a heat transfer press or with an iron at 180°C, for 30sec. Do this carefully and always place some paper on top to protect the fabric from scorching. Take care at this point as the printed fibres will begin to loosen, with the chemical active on it. Once you have finished baking, immediately submerge the fabric in warm water, to wash-out all the loose fibres. If they are proving slightly stubborn, then gently use a nail-brush to brush them out, but be careful not to distort the weave of the fabric left behind.

PROTEIN DEVORÉ

Common fabric mixes are wool/nylon, wool/viscose/nylon, or to burn controlled holes through the fabric, felted wool is best.

For a sample amount of 100g:

- 30g sodium hydroxide (caustic soda)
- cold water, enough to dissolve the sodium hydroxide
- 100g of starch ether (solvitose C5)

1) This process requires a great deal of care, as caustic soda will burn, when mixed with water. Make sure you have strong rubber gloves, mask and eye protection.

2) Using a strong plastic pot, pour in a small quantity of water and stir in the desired amount of caustic soda, using a wooden stick for stirring. At this point the solution will heat rapidly.

3) Add the starch ether, stirring carefully.

4) Print the fabric – heavyweight fabrics may need up to ten pulls for the paste to penetrate through enough.

5) Sometimes the paste will burn through the fabric immediately after printing if you have been able to use the mixture quickly after you have mixed it up. If this has happened then you can wash-out the fabric before the print has dried.

6) Otherwise you will need to print the fabric, leave it to dry, and then steam it for 5min, and this will destroy the protein fibre.

7) You may need to test your steaming times on different fabrics as the solution easily spreads and burns out areas outside your print.

8) The fabric then needs washing in warm water to remove the chemical and printing gum.

LUREX DEVORÉ

A common fabric mix is polyester/lurex (metallic split film).

For a sample amount of 100g:

- 30g sodium carbonate (soda ash)
- cold water, enough to dissolve soda ash
- 100g Indulca

1) Dissolve the sodium carbonate with water, and then stir in the Indulca.

2) Print or paint your image onto fabric, and wait for the print to dry.

3) The fabric will then need steaming for 10min, and the metallic fibre will have dissolved.

4) Wash-out the remaining chemical and printing gum in warm water.

This effect can also be achieved in a boiling dye bath of water, using resist dye techniques (see Chapter 6).

1) Fill a dye bath with enough water to cover your fabric comfortably, and add sodium carbonate directly into the bath.

2) For every 3l of water you will need approximately 50g of soda ash. Dye can also be added at the same time to colour the fabric woven with the metallic fibres.

3) Bring the solution to the boil, and add your fabric tied or clamped to resist areas, and boil for around 15–20min, which should strip out the aluminium film.

4) Do this in a well-ventilated area.

Equipment for Fixing and Finishing

If you are working in a well-equipped textile studio, then you are likely to have access to the best equipment for fixing and finishing your fabrics; if not, there are ways to improvise. Most printing inks need some form of fixation, and not doing this properly will make it difficult to sell printed textile work professionally.

Steaming

A professional textile steamer such as a bullet steamer, gives by far the best results for fixing dyes onto fabrics, and the steaming times will remain constant. Steamers can be bought in different sizes, and the smaller ones can be used with a regular electrical socket.

Steaming times:

Reactives (Procion) – 20min
Acid on nylon – 30min
Acid on wool and silk – 1hr
Discharge – 10min
Protein devoré – 5min
Lurex devoré – 10min
Shaping polyester fabrics – 30min

1) The printed fabric will need to be wrapped in a clean piece of calico to protect it from any water drips in the steamer. For steaming long lengths of fabric, hessian or another cellulose fabric with a loose weave is more suitable, to allow the steam to penetrate through more easily.

2) Lay out the calico, which should be slightly wider than the piece of work, and about 2m longer. Pin your fabric at intervals along the edge, attaching it to the backing cloth.

3) Both fabrics should be rolled or folded in a way to prevent the printed textile being folded against itself, and always having the clean calico in between. This can then be hung in the steamer, so make sure the fabric is folded small enough so that it doesn't touch the base of the steamer.

4) Always wear heat-protective gloves when using a steamer, and regularly clean your backing cloth.

5) On a small scale, a pressure cooker could be used on a portable stove to create the same effect. If you cannot access a steamer, then you will have to air-hang the fabric instead. Leave the fabric to dry slowly overnight in a warm, slightly humid environment, such as a bathroom. This allows the fixation process to continue.

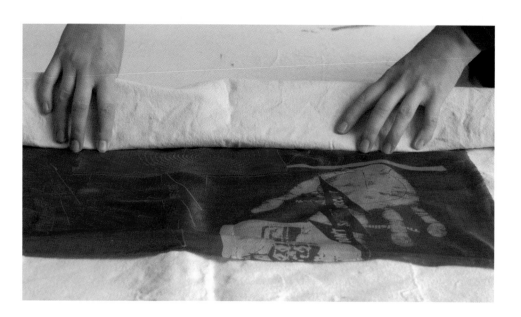

When steaming, roll the fabric in a backing cloth to protect it from water drips.

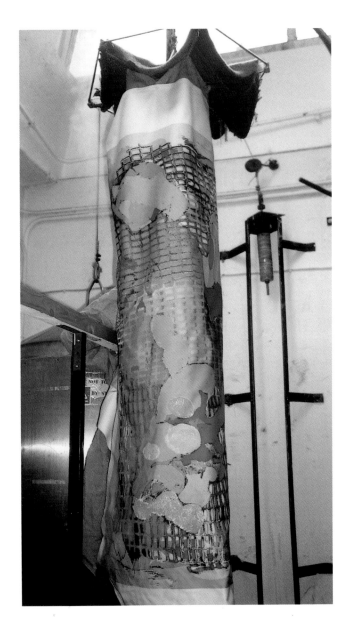

A length of fabric printed with reactive ink on cotton, going into the steamer at Central St Martins College. (Photograph by June Fish)

Baking

A baking cabinet can be used for fixing pigment inks, burning the fibres for cellulose devoré, and moulding synthetic fabrics. It is particularly useful for large-scale pieces of work, but an iron or small heat press will do the same job, on a smaller scale.

Heat Transfer Press and Iron

As well as fixing printing inks and burning out devoré, a heat transfer press or iron is also useful for embossing synthetic fabric, transferring dispersal dyes onto synthetic fabrics (*see* Chapter 3), and sticking adhesives for flock, foil and lamination.

Make sure you protect your press or iron, with Teflon or greaseproof sheets if you are using adhesives or plastic, and newsprint for dye transfers or for the fixing dyes.

Refer to individual recipes for temperatures and timings with a heat press or iron.

These timings may vary according to the type of equipment you have available, so do some tests first.

Washing Out

A large sink or even a bath will be necessary for washing excess dye out of your fabric, particularly for lengths. It is always best to wash the fabric as flat as possible, to avoid the migration of dye from one area to another.

1) Fill the sink or bath with cold water first, and then submerge the fabric; try and avoid having jets of water flowing directly onto one section of the fabric.
2) You will need to be patient, particularly with reactives, because these need a thorough repeated washing.

Once the water has run clear, then you need to wash in hot water, again avoiding a water jet directly hitting the fabric.
3) Metapex detergent is useful for final rinses.

Washing Machine/Spin Dryer

As well as just pre-cleaning your fabric and backing clothes, a washing machine helps give the fabric a final rinse after dyeing or printing, and a spin will quickly show up any printed colours that are bleeding after the first wash, so it can be washed again.

Your machine can also be used for dyeing large pieces of fabric. Make sure you rinse the machine very thoroughly after dyeing.

Never dry any fabric directly on a heat source such as a radiator, or it will be patchy and make the fabric brittle. Ensure that you have a clean space for hanging your fabrics to dry in.

HEALTH AND SAFETY

Before using any of the recipes and materials in Chapters 6 and 7 it is extremely important that you are aware of any potential risks or hazards that could affect your health or cause an accident. This is particularly relevant if you are working at home or in a small studio space where you are using professional workshop equipment, and extra care needs to be taken with the safe use of dyes, chemicals and apparatus. Clean your workshop on a regular basis as this will help keep your equipment in good condition, as well as maintaining a less hazardous environment.

Gather as much information and advice as possible from your supplier or manufacturer on their products, and the purpose you intend to use them for. Assess the environment you are working in to see if it is safe enough for the kind of materials and chemicals you are using (this is called risk assessment), and minimize the risk for any potential accidents. This will be looked at in more detail below.

Safety Data Sheets

By law, your supplier should provide you with a *safety data sheet* for each product you buy at no extra cost, which complies with Government regulations for *COSHH* (*Care of Substances Hazardous to Health*). This will contain any information about the chemical breakdown of the product, possible hazards, first-aid measures, safe storage, handling and disposal.

The safety data sheet will also provide information on personal protection, such as the wearing of gloves, overalls, dust and fume masks and so on, but you will also need to assess your own health on a personal level, to ensure a chemical or dye is safe for you to use. If you suffer from respiratory problems such as asthma, or skin allergies like eczema, then it may

be advisable to avoid products with higher risks, or only use them in a controlled environment or for short periods of time. You may need to consult a doctor for further advice and information, particularly if you are pregnant.

It is recommended that you wear protective gloves, shoes and overalls at all times, and a dust mask (if working with powdered chemicals and dyes).

Hazard Symbols

All chemicals and dyes are labelled with *hazard symbols*. These are generally orange and black in colour (many household cleaning or painting materials have hazard symbols), and show an image representing a potential risk. Listed below:

Flammable (store in a fireproof cupboard)
Explosive (store in a fireproof cupboard)
Oxidizing (can react dangerously with other chemicals)
Harmful/irritant (wear protective gloves, clothing and mask)
Harmful to the environment (dispose of carefully)
Corrosive (will destroy living tissue, so protective clothing, face visor and gloves needed)
Toxic (can cause serious danger to health even at low levels, so avoid completely)

Working Environment

It is also important if you are setting up your own studio space, to ensure that the equipment and facilities available to you are safe to use. If you are buying electrical equipment, discuss with the manufacturer what is the most suitable model for the type of space and existing electrical and water supply available. Issues to look out for:

- Are there enough electrical sockets for all the equipment you require? You need to avoid overloading sockets.
- What type of power supply is needed? Some machinery needs a more powerful electrical supply.
- Is your equipment under guarantee, or can it be regularly serviced?
- Check all flexes and cables are in good condition, and they do not trail loosely over the floor.
- Check that any sinks or washout areas are deep

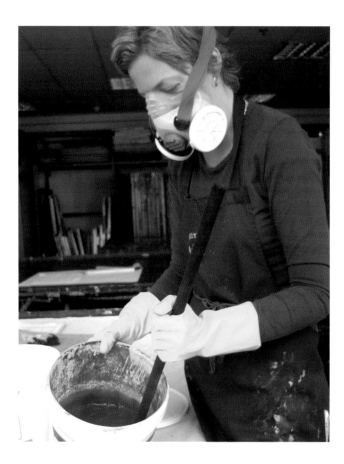

Purchasing a fume mask will spare you the strong odours of many chemicals. Use a fume cupboard for mixing potentially dangerous dyes and chemicals.

enough, and at a safe enough distance from electrical equipment. Or can electrical apparatus be hard wired in, so sockets are not exposed.

- Is there enough ventilation or extraction if you are using strong chemicals? It is recommended that all powdered dyes are mixed in a ventilating cupboard.
- Can you store hazardous chemicals and dyes safely, in a dry, temperate environment. Acids and alkalis generally need to be stored separately.
- If you are using noisy equipment such as a silk-screen wash-out gun, can the noise be insulated properly?

Risk Assessment

Once you have gathered all the information necessary about equipment and materials, then you should make an assessment about its viability in the work space. You may have to find alternative, less harmful products to use, or use them for a shorter period of time, if you do not feel that you have adequate ventilation, storage or power sources. You could source out a professional workshop that will hire out facilities, to enable you to carry out more risky processes in a safer, monitored environment.

Make sure you have a first-aid kit available, and if you are working alone in your own studio space a phone to contact someone if you have an accident. Despite the potential hazards, most common injuries are caused by scalpels and burns from boiling water.

There have been many concerns in recent years about certain dyes and chemicals. If you require any further information on these issues the *Health and Safety Executive* is useful to contact (www.hse.gov.uk).

Disposal of Printing Inks

- Aim to only mix the correct amount of ink (*see* Chapter 7) to avoid waste.
- If this proves difficult, collect the waste in small, tightly sealed tubs, no more than 15kg. Separate the inks into different types, so different chemicals are kept apart.
- It may be possible to arrange with your local council, or a waste disposal company, to remove the waste safely. Do this regularly if need be.

BIBLIOGRAPHY AND SUGGESTED FURTHER READING

USEFUL PUBLICATIONS

American Craft
Artists Newsletter
Crafts
Elle Decoration
International Textiles
Selvedge
Surface Design
Textile Forum
Textile View
Wallpaper
World of Interiors

PRACTICAL INFORMATION

Broughton, Kate, *Textile Dyeing* (Rockport, 1995)
Clarke, W., *An Introduction to Textile Printing* (Butterworths, 1971)
Curtis, Bailey, *Dyeing to Colour* (Bought through Omega Dyes and Bailey Curtis, 2001)
Dunnewold, Jane, *Complex Cloth* (Fibre Studio Press, 1996)
Giles, Rosalie P., *Fabrics for Needlework* (Methuen and Co Ltd, 1964)
Johnston, Ann, *Colour by Design* (Ann Johnston USA, 2001)
Parker Johnston, Meda, Kaufmann Glen, *Design on Fabrics* (Litten Educational Publishing Inc, 1967)
Kendall, Tracy, *The Fabric and Yarn Dyer's Handbook* (Collins and Brown, 2001)

King, Hazel, *Fabric Types* (Oxford Heinemann Library, 2001)
Kinnersley, Joanne, Taylor, *Dyeing and Screen-Printing on Textiles* (A & C Black, 2003)
Knutson, Linda, *Synthetic Dyes for Natural Fibers* (Interweave Press, 1986)
Laury, Jean, *Imagery on Fabric* (C & T Publishing, 1997)
McNamara, Andrea, and Snelling, Patrick, *Design and Practise for Printed Textiles* (Oxford University Press, 1995)
Scott, Jac, *Textile Perspectives in Mixed-Media Sculpture* (The Crowood Press, 2003)
Storey, Joyce, *Fabrics and Dyes* (Thames and Hudson Ltd, 1978)
Tortora, Phyllis G., *Understanding Textiles* (Macmillan, 1982)
Wells, Kate, *Fabric Dyeing and Printing* (Conran Octopus Ltd, 1997)

DESIGN INFORMATION

Braddock, Sarah E., and Mahoney, Marie, *Techno Textiles* (Thames and Hudson, 1998)
Cole, Druisilla, *1000 Patterns* (A & C Black, 2003)
Gale, Colin, and Kaur, Jabir, *The Textile Book* (Berg, 2002)
Itten, J., *Elements of Colour* (Van Nostrand Reinholdt, 1970)
Jackson, Leslie, *20th Century Pattern design* (Octopus, 2002)
Jerstop, Karin, and Kohlmark, Eva, *The Textile Design Book* (Lark Books, 1998)
Lenor Larson, Jack, *Furnishing Fabrics* (Thames and Hudson, 1989)

McDermott, Catherine (ed.), *English Eccentrics* (Phaidon Press, 1992)

Mellor, Susan, and Elfers, Joost, *Illustrated History of Textiles* (Thames and Hudson, 1991)

Wilson, Jaquee, *Handbook of Textile Design* (Woodhead Publishing, CRC Press, 2002)

Iwamoto Wada, Yoshiko, *Memory on Cloth* (Kodansha International, 2002)

Yates, Marypaul, *Textiles: A Designer's Handbook* (W.W. Norton, 1996)

ARTICLES

Crafts Council, *Printed, Painted and Dyed Textiles* (Issue number 5, February 1995)

Textile Magazine, *Natural Dyes: An Eco Solution?* (Issue number 3, 1999)

Textiles Magazine, *Digital Ink Jet Printing of Textiles* (Issue number 1, 2004)

Textile Magazine, *The Road to True Wearable Electronics* (Issue number 1, 2004)

New Scientist *That's Cool* (May 2000)

LIST OF SUPPLIERS

UNITED KINGDOM

Adkins and Sons Ltd:
High Cross,
Lancaster Road,
Hinckley,
Leicestershire LE10 0AW
01455 891291
www.aadkins.com
*New and reconditioned heat transfer presses,
high frequency welding machines*

BA Marketing:
The Studio,
Denford Manor Barn,
Bath Road,
Hungerford,
Berkshire RG17 0UN
01488 686866
www.colourist.info
Heat transfer inks

Colourcraft (C&A) Ltd:
Unit 5, 555 Carlisle Street East,
Sheffield S4 8DT
0114 242 1431
www.colourcraftltd.com
*Dyes, printing inks, speciality inks, batik, drawing
and painting materials, storage containers*

Creative Beadcraft:
Neal Street,
London, W1
www.creativebeadcraft.co.uk
*Beads, sequins, can be ordered wholesale
over the Internet*

Dark Blue Ltd:
Unit K, Trecnydd Business Park,
Trecnydd,
Caerphilly,
Wales CF83 2RZ
02920 859183
webmaster@dark-blue.co.uk.
Sublimation printing and large-scale textile printing

Dykem 2003 Ltd:
71 Paget Road,
Leicester LE3 5HN
0116 2624975
Sells off ranges of dyes and auxiliary chemicals

Dylon International Ltd:
0208 663 4296
www.dylon.co.uk for individual stockists
Range of dyes and dye applications

Fibrecrafts and George Weil:
1 Old Portsmouth Road,
Peamarsh,
Guildford,
Surrey GU3 1LZ
01483 565807
www.georgeweil.co.uk
Dyes, inks and auxiliaries, fabric, equipment
and useful information and recipes

Hiva Products:
2 Disraeli Street,
Aylestone,
Leicester LE2 81X
01162 836977
www.hiva.co.uk
Flock paper (sold only by the roll)

Kemtex Educational Suppliers:
Chorley Business and Technology Centre,
Euston Lane,
Chorley,
Lancashire PR7 6TE
01257 230220
www.kemtex.co.uk
Comprehensive range of dyes, printing inks
and auxiliaries, that can be purchased in
small quantities. Also supply recipe sheets

Maculloch and Wallis:
25–26 Dering Street,
London W1R 0BH
0207 629 0311
www.maculloch-wallis.co.uk
Fabrics, haberdashery and trimmings

Morplan:
56 Great Titchfield Street,
London WIP 8DX
0207 636 1887
Mail order number: 0800 451122
www.morplan.com
Display products and tools for fashion

Pongees:
28–30 Hoxton Square,
London N1 6NN
0207 739 9130
www.pongees.co.uk
Silk fabrics, including silk/viscose devore fabrics
Trade and students only

Quality Colours Ltd:
Unit 13, Gemini Project,
Landmann Way,
London SE14 5RL
0207 394 8775
Comprehensive range of dying and printing materials, which
can be purchased in small quantities

R.A. Smart:
Clough Bank,
Grimshaw Lane,
Bollington,
Macclesfield,
Cheshire SK10 5NZ
01625 576231
www.RASmart.co.uk
Printing and finishing equipment

Screen Colour Systems:
Waterfall Cottages,
Waterfall Road,
Colliers Wood,
London SW19 2AE
0208 241 2050
Printing inks and silk screen equipment

Selectasine Serigraphics Ltd:
65 Chislehurst Road,
Chislehurst,
Kent BR7 5NP
0208 467 8544
Printing inks, silk screens, squeegees, newsprint,
photo emulsion, lamp for photostencil exposure

Sericol:
0845 084 8989
www.sericol.com (for individual stockists)
Range of printing equipment including
flatbed digital printing, and speciality inks

Silk Bureau:
1 Church Cottage,
Ryden Lane,
Charlton,
Worcestershire WR10 3LQ
01386 861122
www.info@silkbureau.co.uk
Digital print services for paper and fabric

Thomas and Vines Ltd:
Units 5 & 6,
Sutherland Court,
Tolpits Lane,
Watford,
Herts WD18 9SP
01923 775111
Range of adhesives for fabrics

Tonertex Foils Ltd:
PO Box 3746,
London N2 9DE
0208 444 1992
info@tonertex.com
Foil papers and glitters

Whaleys (Bradford) Ltd:
Harris Court,
Great Horton,
Bradford,
West Yorkshire BD7 4EQ
01274 576718
www.whaleys.co.uk
Comprehensive range of fabrics, including devore,
dissolvable and dischargeable fabrics

USA

Aljo Manufacturing Co:
81–83 Franklin St,
New York,
NY 10013
212/226-2878
www.aljodye.com
Dyes and auxiliaries, and batik materials

Colorado Wholesale Dye Corp.
1-800-697-1566
www.bestdye.com
Dyes and auxiliaries

Createx Colors:
14 Airport Park Road,
E. Granby, CT 06026
800-243-2712
www.createxcolors.com
Dyes and equipment for dye effects.
General art materials

Dharma Trading Company:
PO Box 150916,
San Rafael, CA 94915
800-542-7657
www.dharmatrading.com
Dyes, inks and printing materials

Dick Blick:
PO Box 1267,
Galesburg, IL 61402
800-828-4548
www.dickblick.com
Screen printing, and general art materials

Jaquard Products:
www.jacquardproducts.com
(check website for shop outlets)
Textile paints and dyes

PhotoEZ:
www.photoezsilkscreen.com
Emulsion for making screen stencils,
and building a light table

The Prairie Fibers Company:
www.prairiefibers.com
Natural dyes and paints

PRO Chemical:
PO Box 14,
Somerset,
MA 02726
0800-228-9393
www.prochemical.com
Dyes and auxiliaries, equipment and written information

Sericol:
www.sericol.com (for individual addresses)
*Silk screens, range of printing equipment,
speciality printing inks*

Silk Connection:
www.silkconnection.com
Range of cotton, viscose, silk and nylon fabrics

Silk Paint Corporation:
18220 Waldron Drive,
PO Box 18,
INT Waldron,
MO 64092
www.silkpaint.com

Standard Dyes, Inc:
PO Box 2808,
01 Brentwood St,
High Point,
NC 27261
336-841-5468
www.standarddyes.com
Dyes and auxiliaries

Testfabrics Inc:
PO Box 26,
West Pittston,
PA 18643
570-603-0433
www.testfabrics.com
Pre-washed fabrics

AUSTRALIA

Batik Oetro:
203 Avoca St,
Randwick,
NSW 2031
www.dyeman.com
Dyes, inks, printing emulsions and batik equipment

Jacquard Products:
www.jacquardproducts.com
(check website for shop outlets)
Textile paints and dye

Kraft Kolour Pty Ltd:
242 High Street,
Northcote,
Victoria 3070
+6139482-9234
www.kraftKolour.com.au
Dyes, inks and printing materials

Marie France:
92 Currie Street,
Adelaide,
SA 5000
Silks, paints and dyes

Sericol:
www.sericol.com (for individual addresses in Australia)
Silk screen, range of printing equipment, speciality inks

USEFUL ORGANIZATIONS

UNITED KINGDOM

ACID:
Adelaide House,
London Bridge,
London EC4R 9HA
www.acid.uk.com
Design protection and legal advice

BRIFFA:
Business Design Centre,
Upper Street,
Islington,
London N1 0QH
0207 288 6003
www.briffa.com
Design protection and legal advice

Chartered Society of Designers:
5 Bermondsey Exchange,
179–181 Bermondsey St,
London SE1 3UW
0207 357 8088
www.csd.org.uk
*Offers portfolio advice, and work placements,
and continuing professional development programme*

Crafts Council:
44a Pentonville Road,
London N1 9BY
0207 278 7700
Gallery, bookshop, resource centre and library
www.craftscouncil.org.uk

London Print Works Trust:
Unit 7,
Brighton Terrace,
London SW9 8DJ
0207 738 7841
www.londonprintworks.com
Hires out workshop facilities, runs courses and exhibitions

Register of Apparel & Textile Designers:
5 Portland Place,
London W1B 1PW
0207 636 5577
www.ukfashionexports.com
*Information and library resource, for members and industry. Plus
support and freelance projects for fashion and textile designers*

The Dover Bookshop:
18 Earlham Street,
London WC2H 9LG
0207 836 2111
www.doverbooks.co.uk
Copyright-free books and images

USA

American Crafts Council Library:
72 Spring St,
NY 10012-4019
212-274-0630
www.craftcouncil.org

AUSTRALIA

Artistcare:
www.craftvic.asn.au
*Lists gallery and shop outlets,
information throughout Australia*

Crafts Council:
www.craftaus.com.au
*Information on galleries, exhibitions,
education and promoting craft makers*
www.ozco.gov.au
Funding and promotional opportunities for craftmakers

INDEX